MANNISHLAWS

by Solomon Christian

What's behind the *Mannishlaws* movement?
It's really incorporated in the term
Mannishlaws itself.
We're talking about man issues, putting them in a set of
rules so that we'll have something to think about when
we experience them.

By men, about men – *Mannishlaws*.

MANNISHLAWS: Manhood Defined
By Solomon Christian

www.mannishlaws.com/products

 www.facebook.com/mannishlaws2019/

 @mannishlaws

 #mannishlaws

Cover Design: Illinoius Christian

Graphics © Pexels.com and UNsplash.com

Published by:

Powell House Creative Services, Louisville KY 40220 USA

tracewriter.wordpress.com

Printed by: Colorstream Digital, Nashville TN

A CIP record for this book is available from the Library of Congress Cataloging-in-Publication Data

ISBN-13: 978-0-578-62263-7

Printed in USA

CONTENTS

INTRODUCTION 9

PART ONE

MANHOOD DEFINED 18

RULE 1.1: You Must be a Male 19

RULE 1.2: You Must Provide 21

RULE 1.3: You Must Protect 23

RULE 1.4: You Must Preserve 23

PART TWO

DEFINING WHO YOU ARE 26

RULE 2.1: Understand Fairness 31

RULE 2.2: Know your Brand 31

RULE 2.3: Set Personal Standards and Expectations 32

RULE 2.4: Set Your Own Agenda 33

RULE 2.5: Make the Hard Decisions 34

RULE 2.6: Define Your Character and Roles 35

RULE 2.7: Have a Dream – It's Free 36

RULE 2.8: Know the Cost of Failure 37

RULE 2.9: Determine What Your Deal Breakers Are 38

RULE 2.10: Recognize the End Game 39

RULE 2.11: Grow by Subtraction When Able 40

RULE 2.12: A Clear Mind is the Foundation for All Growth 42

RULE 2.13: A Static Lifestyle is Unhealthy 44

RULE 2.14: Seek Out What You Don't Know 44

RULE 2.15: Demonstrate Urgency for All Things Urgent 46

RULE 2.16: Create Value With Your Words 47

CONTENTS *(cont.)*

RULE 2.17: Be Ordinary First 48

RULE 2.18: Recognize Your Proclivities 49

RULE 2.19: Denial is Venom 50

RULE 2.20: Be an Advocate for Yourself 50

RULE 2.21: Develop a Proactive Mindset 51

RULE 2.22: Be Self-aware, and Self-accountable 52

RULE 2.23: Don't Marry Yourself to Being Right 53

RULE 2.24: Recognize and Resist the Man Killers 54

RULE 2.25: Develop Sustainable Habits for Growth 55

RULE 2.26: Set Goals, Not Dreams 57

RULE 2.27: Status Can't Be Your Driver 58

RULE 2.28: Fear of Failure is Emotional Paralysis 59

RULE 2.29: You Can't Become a "True Man" Overnight 61

RULE 2.30: Know Your Limits Then Push Them 64

RULE 2.31: Frame Your Own Success 65

RULE 2.32: Know the Givers and Takers 67

RULE 2.33: Overcoming the Survival Mindset 68

RULE 2.34: Just Say HELP 69

PART THREE

WALK LIKE A MAN 72

RULE 3.1: A "True Man" Can't be Held Emotionally Hostage 73

RULE 3.2: Deadbeat Dads 75

RULE 3.3: Life is About More Than Stuff 78

RULE 3.4: Align Your Expectations and Goals 80

RULE 3.5: Don't Get Caught Up in a Bundle 81

CONTENTS *(cont.)*

RULE 3.6: You Must Set Boundaries for Your Friends 84

RULE 3.7: You Can't Kick It With Coworkers 85

RULE 3.8: Mind Your Business 87

RULE 3.9: Just Because You Say It, Doesn't Make It So 89

RULE 3.10: Keep the Main Thing the Main Thing 90

RULE 3.11: You Play to Win 93

RULE 3.12: Don't Condition, Then Complain 95

RULE 3.13: Nine Words of Death 98

RULE 3.14: ""Facetiming"" is Reckless 101

RULE 3.15: No Joint Bank Accounts 103

PART FOUR

RELATING TO WOMEN 105

RULE 4.1: Date for Substance, not Circumstance 108

RULE 4.2: Compatibility Breeds Longevity 109

RULE 4.3: Financial Compatibility is Important 112

RULE 4.4: Create a Culture of Praise and Recognition 113

RULE 4.5: Give Credit When It's Not Due 114

RULE 4.6: Beating Your Chest Will Leave You Sore 115

RULE 4.7: Exercise Grace, Forgiveness and Flexibility 115

RULE 4.8: Care About More Than You 117

RULE 4.9: Do, or Don't. But Stop With All the Trying. 118

RULE 4.10: Don't Justify a Failure 120

RULE 4:11: Never Seek Permission 122

RULE 4.12: Make Your Standard the Deal-breaker 124

RULE 4.13: Don't be Afraid to do Without 125

CONTENTS *(cont.)*

RULE 4.14: Keep the Conflict About the Issue 127

RULE 4.15: Expect Baggage, but Managed Drama 128

RULE 4.16: Set the Parameters of Your Relationship Early 129

RULE 4.17: Clear, Honest Communication is Essential 131

RULE 4.18: Manage your Expectations of Her 133

RULE 4.19: They Will Believe What You Tell Them 136

RULE 4.20: Create a Natural Option for Her 137

RULE 4.21: Own Her Answer 139

RULE 4.22: Constantly Question your Optics 140

RULE 4.23: Intimacy Impacts Expectations 142

RULE 4.24: A Big Tool is Just a Big Tool 143

RULE 4.25: Know Your Net Worth 145

RULE 4.26: Get Yours, Don't Covet Hers 146

RULE 4.27: Don't Insult the Intelligence of a Scorned Woman 148

RULE 4.28: Don't Minimize Her Purpose 151

RULE 4.29: Relationship Congruency 153

RULE 4.30: Relationships Can't be a Struggle 156

RULE 4.31: No Domestic Abuse 157

RULE 4.32: No Male Friends 160

RULE 4.33: You Can't Avoid Difficult Conversations 162

RULE 4.34: No Time for Life 163

RULE 4.35: Love by the Numbers 164

RULE 4.36: Go Slow for What? 165

RULE 4.37: She's Not Your Everything 168

CONTENTS *(cont.)*

PART FIVE

HOW YOU ALLOW HER TO TREAT YOU 170

RULE 5.1: You Can't be an Option 172

RULE 5.2: Her Persuader is Best 178

RULE 5.3: Don't be Led Around by the "Good-Good" 182

RULE 5.4: Respect My Space 184

RULE 5.5: They Are Who They Say They Are 185

RULE 5.6: 50/50 Ain't Good Enough 188

RULE 5.7: No More "First Times" 189

RULE 5.8: You Can't Accept Their Stress 192

RULE 5.9: A Spoiled Woman 195

RULE 5.10: Respect Our Place 199

CONCLUSION 201

INTRODUCTION

This book is written to provide a lifelong guide for progressive, reflective, self-respecting males seeking to achieve a life of happiness, success and general fulfillment for himself, his family and his community. We will explore numerous challenges of true-to-life circumstances and corresponding insight for success in navigating those choppy waters.

Additionally, you will know core concepts that build a solid foundation of manhood that will never crack. I explore many concepts that you'll find yourself referencing often. Post-it Notes and a highlighter will serve you well. We'll begin the journey with a reflection on those who influenced the evolution of my perspectives.

First, we need to ask: What's in a man? Who's to say? Therein lies the problem.

I consider myself blessed and – to some degree – just plain lucky. Blessed, because I had a family unit that was all in for me. In each person's unique way, my parents and maternal grandparents instilled in me a value system that promoted dreaming, working and achieving. I consider myself lucky because even in spite of my many poor life choices, I've been able to achieve some level of sustained success in life. Not financial wealth, not fame or notoriety, but success in terms of building and growing businesses, raising and developing young men, leading and loving families, and positively impacting my immediate community.

My Father

My father, a junior high school resource officer and a semi shell-shocked Vietnam veteran, was a perennial underachiever. He believed in doing his best at whatever he had to do ... so long as it did not cause stress or inconvenience in his life or daily activities.

His lack of vision, or limited attainment, wasn't because he couldn't do any better, it was simply because he was committed to living a minimalist life, a life free from the stress of the "chase" associated with the "catch." It seems like yesterday that I overheard him telling my mother he had experienced a lifetime of stress in "'Nam," and he was leaving it there. So, while this stress-free mindset prevented him from seeking to do more for himself on a professional level, or be more for his family, it did not stop him from doing those things that he enjoyed most. You could count on him being at the Rosecroft Racetrack three nights a week playing the horses. Fridays and Saturdays were the golf days that he relished so much. Sometimes he'd even take me along to struggle with carrying the golf bag for nine holes. Of course he never could play a complete 18 holes, because he only had about nine holes of patience with my complaining and total disinterest in the sport.

My father was the king of "after the fact" teaching. He taught me very little in the way of avoidance or preparation. The onset of his wisdom was always retrospective. The whole "measure twice, cut once" or "the ounce of prevention thing" – no, we'd have none of that. What we did have was a ton of "Son, let this be a lesson to you" or "See, that just goes to show..." speeches after the damage had already been done or the sting of disappointment had set in.

His approach to tackling life challenges and crisis involved finding the easiest or the cheapest solution; the simplest way to get something done. Never the most effective or efficient way, but more times than not, it was simply the cheapest, easiest, least painful way.

Milestone Memory

I'll never forget being upstairs in my room when I heard a disturbing noise. It was a deep, bellowing rumble. I looked outside expecting to see a big truck of some sort, but no, it was just my mom pulling up. You see, we lived up north where the winters were brutal. The snow, ice and salt from the roads could wreak havoc on the best car, and that's exactly what had happened.

On this day the elements delivered a decisive blow to our teal-green 1977 Cutlass Supreme Brougham. The exhaust pipe had corroded and broken in half. Now, a reasonable person would consider taking the car in for repairs. And that's exactly what my mom suggested that my father do. But by now, you (the reader) may have figured that there was nothing reasonable about my old man. His thinking was, "Why would I pay for the car to be repaired when I can fix it myself with everything that I have around this house?"

On this cold winter day, I watched my ole man cut the top and bottom out of a tin soup can and mend the pipe back together with HVAC duct tape. Finished, he cranked the car and it sounded horrendous. He looked at me with a sense of accomplishment and said, "Son, let this be a lesson to you. There is more in the man than there is in the land."

At that moment, I learned a valuable lesson. Not about auto repair, but the spirit of what he was trying to teach me. My father was demonstrating to me that a man does not have to accept life circumstances on the platter that they are served upon. He is greater than his circumstances, so it's up to him to determine how he will respond to life's challenges and crisis.

My Mother

His wife, my mother, is a retired elementary teacher and spiritually grounded woman who has an uncanny ability to tie all things back to her emotional strength or her love for Christ. All my life I remember her as being a sickly woman. One infection to the next, a second operation to the third, in and out of the hospital from time unending. These debilitating health issues were a result of the physical and emotional strife she had experienced as a child, or at least that's how she explains it to me. Even now, on the shortest of phone calls, I can count on hearing that "God" made her so strong because he knew what hardships she'd have to endure in life.

Growing up, she smothered me with love and attention – so much so that, as I began to mature and develop dating relationships, her involvement in various areas of my life became problematic. Through the years, our relationship has been strained on many occasions because of my failure to accommodate her level of need for involvement in some of the more private areas of my life. I remember once, during a heated argument, I even went so far as to remind her that we were not dating.

But even still, valuable lessons were taught and learned. Most notably, boundaries and expectations. Though inadvertently, through our relationship, as well as how I observed her life, My mother taught me the importance of setting clear boundaries and managing the expectations of self and others. She helped me understand the value in discerning who to let in and who to keep out.

My Grandfather

My grandfather was a minister with a 7th-grade education. He could find a lesson to teach me from watching two ants walk across the ground. Even though his formal education was limited, he was always achieving things, always acquiring the ability to prosper at higher and higher levels in life. He was a hustler of sorts. Not by doing something wrong, or being involved in something illegal or immoral, but a hustler in the sense of always seeking the next opportunity to elevate. One of the things that I admired most about him was the energy he invested in others so that they could have better opportunities to prosper as well.

Not a single day has passed since his death that I have not thought about him. He will always be my hero.

As a youth, one of his greatest teachings took place while we were changing a starter on a 1977 Ford LTD. My grandfather was talking to me about manhood. How a man must be responsible; how he must have his own things and hold himself accountable. He told me to look at the ground and tell him what I saw. I responded, "Dirt, grass, pine straw... I don't know." He told me to look again and concentrate. So I stared at the ground for a while, to the point I even started getting light-headed.

He asked again, "Do you see anything?"

"Just some ants," I responded.

He then asked, "What are they doing?"

"I don't know ... dragging something."

He said, "Exactly. The ants have more sense than men. They toil hard and struggle in the sun. When the rain comes the ants will be inside, but you won't be. You'll be in the rain struggling, trying to earn your keep."

My Grandmother

Then there was his wife, my grandmother, the matriarch. She was the oldest of 16. A naturally confrontational and defiant woman, she was a "Do as I say do, or else" kind of woman. I only chose the "Or else" option a few times. And on those occasions she quickly helped me feel the error of my choice. Her favorite utensil was a switch off the peach tree in the backyard, which she referred to as "the persuader."

Her strictness was matched only by the love and affection that she frequently demonstrated.

I never knew so many household chores and homeopathic remedies even existed. And then there was the cooking – frying, baking, boiling, steaming, grilling and smoking. Virtually anything that could be done to food was done in her kitchen or on her back porch.

She was a peculiar type of woman with a level of disdain for women of my generation that I just could not understand. She would often say to me, "These women ain't hittin' on shit. They're only good for one thing. If she screws you good, expect an unkept house. If she works, she will always be too tired to screw you or keep house. If she keeps house well, then you can bet she's screwing the neighbor." She'd then go on to say, "Boy... it's up to you to know what you need most and who to get it from.

That's why I'm doing my very best to prepare you to only need a woman for that one thing." Unfortunately, at that time, my lack of maturity would not allow me to fully comprehend her messages. But now I'm a man and I understand her testimony.

The Takeaway(s)

So again I'll say, I'm blessed and definitely lucky. My family values, my life experiences, as well as the things that I have observed from others have taught me much in my development. But there remains one question that still leaves me challenged and perplexed from conversation to conversation ...

What exactly is a man?

When I talk with friends, guys I know at the barbershop, at church, and in other social circles, we often use the word "Man" as a generally accepted term, and we expect for everyone to know exactly what we mean. And we kind of do. We'll say things like, "Man look, sometimes you gotta man up," or "You just gotta be a man," and then there's the famous "A man's gotta do what a man's gotta do." Yet, what exactly does the word "Man" mean? If we just accept the term Man with no standard or qualitative definition or level of exactness, how do we grow, understand, or correct things that aren't right with what we believe?

So, with these recurring questions and thoughts about manhood pressing on my psyche, I committed to taking on the challenge of writing a book, hoping I can help establish a better baseline for people to understand what it is to be a man, as well as how to use the term intelligently. I call this book *Mannishlaws* because what is shared is a combination of rules, observations and principles that, when put together, form laws.

Even so, it is important that you understand that, as I seek to define manhood, no contrast will be made to speak to the morality of man. There will be no good man versus bad man, gay men versus straight man, weak man versus strong man, or white man versus black man. There will simply be a conversation about the male and his opportunity to become a man – the things that separate the man from everyone else.

PART ONE

MANHOOD DEFINED

I'm a grown-ass man.

If I've heard this statement once, I've heard it a million times. What's always perplexed me the most is why anybody would feel the need to state what should be obvious to others, at least physically. I mean really, what scenario is there that a male over the age of 21 would feel the need to affirm that he is a man to anyone, except in cases where people fail to recognize his behavior as being that of such.

Hmmm ... that's a thought.

Our most basic challenge is in understanding what separates a man from an adult male, a nice guy, an oversized adolescent, or someone that just walks around with the male genitalia. What exist are several factors. First, we must understand that a man is known by what he does, just as much as by what he does not do. Not only this, but he has an ability to recognize and embrace certain actions that should be taken – or avoided – and he's able to accept that responsibility and fulfill any requirements that arise. Now, that's saying a lot by itself. But there's even more. We can go on and on with specific traits, and characteristics that we would like to see in a man, but then we start moving from the quantitative descriptions of manhood to the qualitative ones. But at this moment, that's just not our goal. Right now, for the purposes of this book, we need to define the term "man" on the most basic level.

Part One will lay down the fundamental principles of manhood. If you are unable to adhere to these principles on a consistent basis, you cannot consider yourself a man, at least not by the *Mannishlaws* definition. You may complete this book and find benefit in it. And if you do, you're certain to become a better you. But, you still won't be a man. This you must work on.

RULE 1.1: You Must be a Male

I can't tell you how many times I've heard people, mostly women, say that having a penis doesn't make you a man. Typically I hear this comment in some instance where someone is trying to devalue the role of a man, or exert some type of pressure on the man to reach an outcome that's more desirable for the commenter.

While I do agree that a penis doesn't make you a man, I also say from a purely physical aspect, you must have the anatomy of a male to be a man. In no uncertain terms can you be a man without this characteristic. Now saying this, I know there's going to be somebody out there that will have a unique experience, maybe a childhood issue or birth defect that brought them into the world with a unique circumstance. I'm not speaking to those people. I'm speaking to the other 99.9997% of the population.

Please understand this – I don't say these things to diminish the struggles or accomplishments of any individual. I simply make this claim, and state it to be rule number one, because all things in this book spring forth from it. This is the most important rule! I don't care what you identify yourself as, if you do not have the anatomy of a male, you cannot be a man. If we fail to accept this, we'll have women, girls and anything else proclaiming themselves as men, to a greater degree than we already see happening.

I can't begin to count the number of conversations I've had directly, or observed, when a female attempts to falsely validate their role as a man. It goes something like this - The woman is the head of a single parent home doing everything that's required to keep the house afloat. Working two jobs, perhaps going to school at night. She's trying to better herself and provide a future for her kids. In the midst of the conversation, she'll tend to make a statement similar to this:

"I take care of my house and my kids by myself. No man around. When something needs to be done, I find a way to do it. I'm the mama and daddy. I'm the woman, and the man. My kids don't need anything that I am not equipped to provide."

When I hear things like this, I often experience a brief level of admiration for the ladies that are talking. But, this admiration is quickly overtaken by the contempt I have for the foolishness they speak.

It is simply absurd to hear a woman say that they are not only Mom, but they're Dad, they're not just the woman, but the man too. It is ridiculous on so many levels. How can anyone think that in the absence of something, you can become that something, even when you do not possess the core characteristics of that missing something?

I think we'd all agree that it would be senseless for a single-parent man, to think that just because he is taking care of his kids in the absence of a woman, that now he can say that he's also the woman, that he is also the mom. And while this mindset is unrealistic and disrespectful on so many levels, we have women saying these things on a daily basis.

RULE 1.2: You Must Provide

You must be able to provide the fundamental life requirements for yourself as well as those you are directly responsible for. This means that you must have developed the capacity to provide shelter for yourself, independent of the need for others' assistance. You must also be able to provide the supporting elements such as food and utilities. With these come life requirements such as being able to manage your financial affairs and responsibilities.

Let's put into real-life context. I know a middle-aged guy. Over the course of his life, he has had an unnatural, unbalanced love affair with money. This love and need for money has always led him to be involved in high-risk illegal activity, abusive relationships, and an undesired association with law enforcement and incarceration.

While he has seen millions of dollars pass through his hands, he is ill-equipped to take care of himself independently on any level. He can't open a bank account on his own. He's not able to get a credit card. He can't lease an apartment in his name. He definitely can't finance, lease or even rent a car. He can't even buy an airline ticket with a credit card or debit card.

The most basic things people do, for him to do, requires the participation and benevolence of someone else. Not only that, he even brags about how he's going to have a woman take care of him in some capacity. His sentiment: "I'm going to have this girl bringing me clothes and food. Going to have another girl taking care of putting money in my pocket. He has it all figured out."

Wrong!

Everything he has, from the lease on his apartment, to the ability that he has to pay his rent, is based on the benevolence of the women he's involved with. This guy provides nothing, but takes everything. If at any point these self-esteem-defected women where to have a change of heart and decided not to be bothered with him, he's in a situation where he could easily be out in the cold, broke, or both. Furthermore, because he hasn't demonstrated an ability to provide for himself, how can he provide for anyone else in a relationship?

RULE 1.3: You Must Protect

Safety (security) is a basic human need. In fact, this need transcends our species. Humans, as well as animals, on a basic level require a certain level of protection and always look to find a place of safety and refuge, and not necessarily in the sense of predator versus prey. You may not always be on guard against an intruder breaking into your home at 12 a.m., or a mugger attacking you on the street, but protection and safety is a feeling experienced when you have organized your life so that you have a sense that allows you to develop, perform and expect better things.

Are you able to provide a feeling of physical and emotional safety and protection for yourself as well as the people you're responsible for? Not only that. Are you able to protect the materialistic things that you have accumulated? Do your life choices create an environment for you to grow and thrive?

RULE 1.4: You Must Preserve

I've often heard people say it's not enough to acquire or to achieve, it is just as necessary to maintain. This is supremely important because much in life is outside the realm of acquiring or losing. A substantial amount of our life accomplishments will come from our ability to preserve and cultivate, and in some cases, what we can pass on to others. It's not always enough to gain, if you don't have the ability to preserve; by just living to gain, you will always find yourself striving, achieving, but ultimately realizing nothing. A lot of effort, for minimal return.

For example, in my childhood a very close friend of mine had a gift relating to numbers. He could look at numbers and spot relationships between things that nobody else would even give a second look. Over time, he found himself excelling at things like gambling and the stock market. Understand that when I was young, the stock market was printed in the newspaper, so you had to look up and down rows and columns of symbols and numbers which would be taxing on the eyes of the normal human being. But this person – we'll call him Larry – just had a gift. He would identify things without even clearly understanding them, and in time he was able to parlay this gift into quite a few money-making ventures. Ultimately, though, Larry's gifts were his curse.

Throughout his life he was constantly finding ways to make money, but he was unable to put into place behaviors and the structure that would allow him to save and preserve what he had accumulated. So, while Larry represents the very first millionaire I've known, he also represents the very first homeless person that I've personally known.

So, I'll ask again, "What is a man?" The answer: an adult male who has developed the capacity to provide, protect and preserve the basic necessities that life requires, for him and those for whom he is responsible, independently of any sustaining assistance from others.

These four rules represent the cornerstone of *Mannishlaws*. All laws, rules and guidelines going forward will rise from these.

PART TWO

DEFINING WHO YOU ARE

When you look in the mirror, who do you see? I mean, outside of your general appearance, are you happy with who you see? If so, then why? If not, why not? Moreover, what exactly is it about your reflection that makes you feel how you feel? When you figure out the answer to that question, then you'll know what, if anything, you need to seek to change in your life.

I strongly believe that there is a direct correlation between how a man treats himself, treats others, and allows others to treat him. Moreover, a man that has vision, goals, dreams, and ambition will present himself in a way that will create opportunities that are vastly different than the man that simply seeks to survive. So, now that we're sure that every man is a male, but every male is not a man, we must also recognize that even among men, there exists opportunities to be good, better and best in our individual lives. Again, not in a moral sense, but with respect to manhood development. Yes, you may be able to provide, protect and preserve. But at what level? Are you just getting by, or thriving? If you are not where you want, or need to be, what's your plan to get there?

If you were to line up 10 men, and ask them, "By any standard of measure, would you like to be successful?" I submit, that 10 out of 10 men would say, "Yes... yes I want to be successful."

But even by their individual measures of success, how many will actually attain it? And while that answer is debatable, go around and asks a handful of people if they consider themselves to be successful and see how many absolute yeses you'll get.

In my research, my discussions with men have shown me that success, attainment or achievement seems to be, in many cases, a nebulous and highly elusive thing. A common theme is that many people equate success with a dream. And more times than not, this is the case because we don't know how to create tangible pathways to get us from where we are, to those things that we have framed a success. This is true regardless of what we call success. Your success may involve developing a new relationship, starting a new business, recovering from an addiction or an incarceration, repairing your credit, or just overcoming poor life choices. When we learn how to develop plans that systematically move us closer to success, we are then able to positively impact our lives and the lives of those that we are responsible for. So, going forward in this section, I want to speak to some of the things that I believe will ultimately have an additive effect on your ability to be able to operate as a man on a higher level.

Understand this: Success is not very hard to find. But only you know what your success looks like. Once you figure out the path to what you want to accomplish, the journey begins. I liken it to a high-priced call girl. She (success) will go home with whomever spends the time and applies the resources that she requires. She doesn't care what you look like, how tall you are, what type of clothes you wear, the color of your skin, or any other descriptors. All she wants to know is that you are committed to giving her the time and attention that she requires.

I'm speaking in these terms because it really boils down to knowing who you are, where you are, and ultimately where you want to be. Knowing these things sets us up to build roadmaps to becoming greater achievers than we are now. This, in turn allows us to know how to properly treat ourselves.

I have never believed that you can compartmentalize behavior, or habits over time. In fact, those things that I do in the living room will, at some point, make their way into the bedroom or the kitchen. Likewise, the way I treat myself is going to shape how I treat others, and how I allow others to treat me. In our discussion of manhood, a lot goes into how an individual male views himself from the standpoint of who they are, what they want to be, and the growth that is required to travel the distance between the two positions.

Now, let's talk about the groups most men fall into, based in part from my experiences, as well as from observations that I've made over the course of building this book.

There's the group of guys that have absolutely no idea what they want to accomplish in life. And, in most cases, they have no defined goals. With this group, day-to-day survival is basically the protocol. Their goal is to simply make it through today – that's success to them.

Next, you have the men who understand where they are, and indeed have dreams and aspirations to do a range of things. But they won't follow through, because when they see the work required to move them from where they are, to where they want to go, they get frustrated and overwhelmed, and find themselves doing nothing. Still, they hold onto those dreams, and every opportunity they get they'll tell you what they're going to do "one day." But with every passing day, "one day" gets even further away from reality.

Then we have a group of individuals that have the worst sense of self-awareness possible. They have visions of things they want to accomplish, things they believe in. They believe they know who they are and where they are, but they're not even close in their assessment. This group sees themselves in a way that's not totally accurate. As a result, they often view their opportunities for accomplishing things on a grand scale. A scale which tends to be out of line with the sum of their resources and abilities.

Day in, and day out, they work hard, but their sleep is often anguished because they're unable to bring their dreams into reality. They often make progress, but not enough to inspire them to overcome the financial and emotional fatigue that comes from burning out chasing a goal that they may likely never reach. Why? Because their poor sense of self-awareness has them building a pathway to success from a nonexistent origin. It's like buying an airline ticket on a flight departing Washington for Los Angeles. You sit in the airport for days waiting on them to call your flight. Frustration builds to a boiling point until you go to the counter and ask when your flight is going to leave, and the attendant tells you the flight is from Washington to Los Angeles – you're in Philadelphia.

Lastly, you have a group that clearly knows where they are, and are actively moving to where they want to be. These are the doers. This group is my favorite, not simply because they do, but because many of the people in this group, at some point, had been a part of the other groups mentioned before. But something caused them to recognize their shortcomings and circumstances (and opportunities), and inspired them to rise above them. Whether they were someone that had no goals and no vision, or someone that had the vision and poor self-awareness, something happened to cause them to see things more clearly and develop a plan to move toward the success they desire.

As previously stated, I've never been one to believe in sustained compartmentalization. I just don't believe that you can have sustained behavior, repetitive behavior, in one part of your life without it affecting other facets. And if you agree with that point, then you will certainly understand that there is a connection between how you treat yourself, how you treat others, and how you allow others to treat you. This leads me to the next battery of rules that speak to how men treat themselves.

RULE 2.1: Understand Fairness

Some say that life is not fair. Nothing could be further from the truth. Life cares about no one, and respects no one. It feels no guilt for the circumstances that it places on anyone, and it doesn't care whether you can bear them or not. Life is definitely fair, just not equitable. So yes, while life disrespects everyone equally, it does not give everyone the same starting point, resources, or circumstances.

As you mature in manhood it is essential that you understand that life, itself, is an adversary of the ignorant and unprepared. So, constantly seek knowledge relating to the things that are important in reaching your goals. Also be in the habit of preparing for, and anticipating challenges that will be along your path.

RULE 2.2: Know Your Brand

In a perfect world, we all will be judged by what we have inside and what we have to offer. You know, the "content of your character" thing. Unfortunately, that's just not the case. We are constantly seen and judged by

strangers, as well as by our friends and associates. Your brand represents the uniqueness of how you present yourself verbally and non-verbally.

Before you have an opportunity to establish a relationship with anyone on any level, your brand starts to speak. It includes the way you wear your clothes, the dialect in which you talk, the verbiage that you choose when you talk, as well as the people that you associate with. Your brand involves virtually anything that can allow people to form an opinion of you.

This being said, it's important to know your brand. What's more, you must also understand that your brand is not necessarily what you say it is – it's what everyone else recognizes it to be. It is also important to understand that whether good or bad, accurate or inaccurate, your brand will also be susceptible to stereotypes. For this reason it's important to remain self-aware and manage your life activities in a way that creates more favorable options and opportunities for you, than barriers.

RULE 2.3: Set Personal Standards and Expectations

Standards and expectations are real. They exist in all aspects of life. Whether at work, at school, or at play, standards exist to manage outcomes. They also serve as filters to screen out those things that should be, from all that should not. But too often, we look to abide by the standards set by others. As you mature in manhood, you must become comfortable setting standards and expectations for yourself.

Not only that, you must be disciplined enough to hold yourself accountable, and have a demonstrated capacity to self-regulate. Your personal standards and expectations will go a long way to bolster your brand. The people who are acquainted with your brand will also know your standards.

RULE 2.4: Set Your Own Agenda

Every day we're exposed to circumstances that require us to take unplanned courses of action. In these situations, it's not uncommon for one action to set the stage for subsequent follow-up actions to be required. Before you know it, you have a range of processes in motion, all unplanned and usually involving a lot of inconvenience and misallocated time. You now have a "de facto agenda" – an actual system, or list of activities, put in motion by various life circumstances, circumstances that have overpowered your initial plans or just filled in otherwise idle time. This "de facto agenda" will often have you exhausting valuable time and effort on activities that have little, to nothing to do with what you ultimately want to accomplish.

Your time will find a home! If you don't plan it wisely now, you're not going to have the time on hand that you'll need later. Because of this, it's imperative that you use as much of your available time on activities that are going to move you closer to your goals. So, whether on a yearly, quarterly, monthly, weekly or daily timeframe, you must set your personal agenda to ensure that you are constantly moving forward, constantly developing, constantly becoming more experienced at whatever you are ultimately trying to do.

At the end of the day, if you don't set your own agenda, circumstances will.

RULE 2.5: Make the Hard Decisions

Decisions are served up on plates of all sizes and shapes. Today's toughest decision might be deciding to go left or right when we reach the fork in the road ahead. But, tomorrow I may be deciding whether to do chemotherapy (or not), and what will happen as a result. These decisions swing wildly from one end of the spectrum of severity to the other, with real life and death results. As men, we must become comfortable with not only making the decisions, but also riding out the consequences.

Of course, we know that all decisions don't come down to yes and no, right and wrong choices. Sometimes it's a matter of degrees; the most of a good thing, or the least of a bad thing. In any case, as a man you must be comfortable making these decisions so that you can advance in life, as well as lead others who depend on you. What you'll find is, as life goes on and relationships develop, the people in your life will look to you for the answers when things go awry. Yet, in these cases, you still may not necessarily have the right answer, or the best answer, but what nobody wants to hear, or see, is your indecision.

Context: Smelling smoke, a woman gets up in the middle of the night and goes downstairs to investigate. Halfway down the stairs, she's overcome with smoke as fire is everywhere. She gathers herself and crawls back up the stairs. Frantically, she wakes her husband up, yelling, "What are we going to do, the house is on fire!" He looks at her with a blank expression and responds, "I don't know, what do you think we should do?"

What happens next is anybody's guess, but it's safe to say that when critical situations arise, one has to be able to make a decision.

Even when your decision is subpar, there will be indicators, usually obvious, to point you in another direction. But, to make no decision, will often leave you in a perilous state.

RULE 2.6: Define Your Character and Roles

Our character reflects the mental, emotional and moral qualities that are distinctive to us. These are comprised of many things, including:

- How we respond under pressure;

- What we do when no one's looking;

- What we do and say when we feel threatened;

- How we respond when we see an opportunity; and

- What we say and do when winning and losing is on the line.

It's simply not enough to have a belief system or limits, or even personal guidelines. They must be outwardly recognizable so that people have an expectation of what you believe and how you will respond when things run counter to your belief system.

As the saying goes, if you don't stand for something, you'll fall for anything. In that same vein I like to say if you don't define your character and your roles in life, others will do so eagerly. But how do we do this? The answer is: re-define your character constantly and consistently. Defining your character means taking a stance regardless of the favorability of the outcome. For instance, if you don't drink Diet Coke, don't order Diet Coke just because your boss does when he takes you to dinner – don't do it just to impress him.

The character of a man should create more opportunities for success, than barriers that restrict him.

RULE 2.7: Have a Dream - It's Free

My grandfather would often say that it's a poor man that doesn't have a dream. I never really understood what he meant by it, until I grew up. Then it all made sense.

Dreams are free. There's no cost, no labor, no work involved in having one. So, everyone can have one, or many. Now, even though they're free, dreams can be extremely valuable, because they're often the breeding ground for great things. Your greatest success could start as a dream, and then at some point you ask yourself, "Why can't this be real?" You challenge yourself and eventually you see that, if not all of the dream can be realized, maybe portions of it can be attained. So you work, and work, and work, and plan, eventually realizing that this thing that was once a dream is now a goal, and you have a new dream because you've figured out how to accomplish the previous one. Given the right resources, what starts as dreams can be transformed into goals that are attainable.

I can't tell you how many stories I've heard of people that grew up in circumstances where they could only dream of having a nice car, a big walk-in closet, or a sizable home. When they were dreaming it, their life perspective did not allow it to be a conceivable reality. But as they matured, they found that these dreams were very much within reach. Transforming these dreams into reality allows new dreams to emerge. So again, dreams are free, and dreams are necessary.

RULE 2.8: Know the Cost of Failure

Consider this: You have a dollar and you lose 10% of it. Now you have 90 cents. Now let's just say you work hard and you gain 10% back. Now you have 99 cents. What happened? You lost 10% and you worked hard to gain the 10% back, but you still aren't where you started from. This is important to understand because when you lose, or fail, you have to work much harder to recover and have the momentum to just catch up.

For this reason it is always critical to calculate the cost of missing your target on the front end, so that you know whether you have the ability to recover should things not go well.

"How much time and money am I willing to spend on this date? What if we don't click?"

"What is the investment required to start my own Gourmet Pig Feet Restaurant? What if it flops? Is this a viable concept?"

There is certain to be risks and costs associated with virtually anything that we undertake. In some cases, the risks or costs will be attached to our failure to act. And though we can't always eliminate the risk, we have to be able to calculate risk and minimize the cost.

As you grow in manhood, you will learn that your successes will be built on your failures. Because of this, it is important that the accumulated costs of your past failures do not outweigh any foreseeable successes.

RULE 2.9: Determine What Your Deal Breakers Are

We know that both success and failure come with a cost – the cost of doing and achieving versus the cost of failing and missing the mark. But before you even get started on your next big plan, you must determine what your breaking point is. At what point are the costs too high? When are the risks far too great for me to consider this plan, or stay on this course? These are your deal breakers.

Not only do you need to identify what your deal breakers are, but you need to identify them before you get involved in what you are planning to do. Only then can you have a fair benchmark, a relative view of what your limit should be. This does not necessarily mean you have a static limit, or breakpoint; it could be a qualitative limit.

For example:

• If I have to pay for a warranty on this car, that's a deal breaker, I'm not buying this car.

- If she can't be faithful, that's a deal breaker. I can't be in a relationship with her.

- If I can't work this job, and go to night school, that's a deal-breaker. I'm going to have to find another job.

- If they don't agree to give me a raise, or stock options, I've got to leave this organization.

- If this situation stops being fun, then I won't continue to participate.

Identifying your deal-breakers is huge,. but it's not the only thing. You must hold yourself accountable to follow through if the deal breaker is tripped. If you say it's a deal breaker but don't treat it as such, not only is it truly not a deal breaker, but you have damaged your ability to be self-accountable.

RULE 2.10: Recognize the End Game

It all comes to an end at some point. Then what are you to do?

Your job – one day you'll retire or get fired. Your relationship – either you break up, or one of you will die. That lovely car you have – it'll eventually wear out; the question is, what will you do when the time after "now" arrives. What is your Plan B? How long do you plan to do what you are doing?

A good friend of mine has been a playboy as long as I've known him. From when we first met back in the late '80s, to this very day, he's prided himself in his skillfulness in playing the ladies. Well, as you may imagine, a lot has changed. His career has taken off, and his head has gained a lot of grey. He's traveled the world and seen a lot, but the unavoidable point is that he has fewer days in front of him, than he has behind him. Yet, he still finds himself in the same transient type relationships. So what will he do when he can't play the women anymore, or be the playboy that he once was? How will he fill that void? What does his life look like in its next chapter? What is his endgame?

Knowing your endgame is extremely important, because it sets the stage – or it should set the stage tomorrow – for what you are chasing today. If chasing women is your thing, when, or how will you know if you've caught the right one? But this rule extends far beyond women. It simply means that on a daily basis, your life activities and pursuits should be working together to create the outcomes that you hope for in the future.

RULE 2.11: Grow by Subtraction When Able

Over my years I've learned that you can't speak wisdom into foolish people. It just does not make sense to them, and it doesn't make sense to continue to try. These people are always going to be interested in and drawn to silliness. You'll find yourself pulling your hair out trying to figure out why common sense does not resonate with them.

Likewise, when we become introspective and honest with ourselves, we should be able to identify certain undesirable characteristics or behaviors that we'd benefit from shedding. Toxic habits, character defects, or addictive tendencies are all anchors that slow us down or even keep us static. When we acknowledge these behaviors, and sever relationships with them, we grow by subtraction.

We grow by reducing the amount of physical and emotional weight that we carry in our daily lives.

Now, some things that we're involved with – whether it's people, addictive tendencies or toxic habits – can't be weaned from. You have to simply walk away, drop it cold turkey.

This reminds me of a friend of mine that met a very pretty woman. This woman was a 10 by most measures. She was attractive, intelligent, and well-spoken. Unfortunately, she was even more devious, possessive and vindictive. My friend loved this woman very much, but regrettably his love for her would not allow him to see that he was being used and manipulated on a regular basis.

He'd break up with her, only for them to be seen together weeks or months later. He tried counseling, as well as communicating his needs to her in various ways, to no avail. Eventually he found that no amount of talking, persuading, begging or pleading was going to help. He also found that he was emotionally entangled with this woman; he felt like he was under her spell. His only option for his personal well-being was to simply walk away. No goodbyes, no last tries, no forwarding phone number or address. And that's exactly what he conjured up the courage to do. He just walked out of her life. Though it took some time, he found that it was one of the best decisions that he could have ever made. Now he's happily married with a family. He was able to recognize that he couldn't negotiate those circumstances. He finally owned his many deal breakers and grew through subtraction.

RULE 2.12: A Clear Mind is the Foundation for All Growth

When I'm coaching young guys I often tell them that Mother Nature, life, gives us all an equal amount of talent. Unfortunately, it's not going to give us an equal amount of ambition to achieve the goals that we set in front of us. So, understanding these things, we must put ourselves in the best position to be successful. Even still, before we can start talking about planning strategies for success, we have to have some idea of what success means to us on a personal level.

But wait, there's more. Before you can begin thinking on the possible accomplishments that are out there waiting on you to slay, you've got to make room mentally. You must create space to be able to process the things that you hope to accomplish.

What does this mean?

It's simple. To be able to visualize a plan, and then execute it, you must have a sense of focus, mental commitment, and a clear thought pattern. Take for example my uncle Johnny.

By all accounts, Johnny's probably one of the world's most useless human beings. Well, he may be good for something besides getting high and smoking crack. But whatever that something is, nobody else has identified it. I raised Johnny up in this example because of a conversation we once had.

I asked my uncle, "Hey, if you weren't high, what would your dreams be?"

He looked at me kind of puzzled.

I said again, "What would you be doing if you weren't always high?"

He pondered my question for a few seconds and then said, "Man, I don't know. I never really thought about it."

I then responded, "You are almost 60 years old, and you have no idea what you could do with a sober mind?"

"No I don't."

I didn't state the obvious – that maybe there's no reason for him ever to be sober. My point was – and is – he had no vision, no dreams, no aspirations on any level. A clear mind probably wasn't going to benefit him anyway. But for those of you that want something, you're going to have to achieve clarity on a consistent basis to put yourself in a position to execute whatever requirements are necessary.

RULE 2.13: A Static Lifestyle is Unhealthy

Life is constantly moving and evolving. Every day brings a new level of change and complexity. Physically, and emotionally speaking, exercise is an essential activity. Physically, a life of static or low-routine behavior does not stress the body enough to keep it performing optimally. If you run three miles on a daily basis, that becomes routine – there comes a point when you are not challenging your body. And over time that will not be exercise anymore. Eventually you'll have to run four or five miles to do your body any good.

It's the same with mental exercise. If you don't expose your mind to a newer, evolving array of information, you will not have the developmental opportunities that you need to keep up with an ever-changing world. Your scope of intellect will be limited, as will your opportunities. So, to obtain a healthier life, become involved with activities that challenge you both physically and mentally.

RULE 2.14: Seek Knowledge and Run From Foolishness

This is the Information Age. We have more resources at our fingertips that can give us knowledge and perspective than at any other time in history. But what do we do with it?

Your goals and dreams are absolutely useless if you are not committed to gaining the knowledge necessary to bring them into fruition. You should be challenging yourself with questions like:

- What do I have that I can use to ... ?

- What else do I need to do today to ... ?

- Who can I ask for, or where can I find help to ... ?

When you decide what your goals are, questions that begin like the ones listed above will lead you down a path of answers that will force you to become more self-aware. Once you know where you are, and what you have to work with, it now becomes all about planning and execution. But you must be fully committed to seeking credible knowledge, as well as the resources needed for you to grow, and accomplish the goals you have in mind.

Now, along the way you're going to encounter fact-less noise, distractions and opportunities for detours. Foolishness – it's all around us. And what you'll find is that, the more you seek knowledge, the more clearly you'll recognize nonsense. Turn the other way, and don't try to engage it. You'll have to ask yourself how much benefit is it to you in dealing with the uninformed, and the distractions they offer?

Ignorance is bliss, until it's not. What you don't know can indeed hurt you, or adversely impact you on so many fronts. Whether professionally, in your relationship, or in a range of other settings, your lack of knowledge in a specific area can render you unable to perform, contribute, or take advantage of an opportunity. A lack of knowledge can limit your very ability to even recognize opportunities to grow, or circumstances that could be to your detriment.

So, to minimize, or at least reduce the opportunity for an ignorance-based calamity to set you back, strive to cultivate relationships that can offer you exposures that you would not have otherwise experienced. Seek mentors and advisors that can share some level of wisdom or create exposures and experiences that will be beneficial to your development.

RULE 2.15: Demonstrate Urgency for All Things Urgent

Everything can't be the most important thing, nor can every fire be a four-alarm fire. That being said, you have to learn to demonstrate an ability to prioritize things. But not only prioritize, but execute in accordance with the levels of importance that you have in front of you.

It's a funny thing – many of us have routines and face high-priority issues. And likewise, many of us find it challenging to address some of our highest-priority issues, yet we have time to complete nearly every "high desire" task. What happens when we get in the habit of foregoing the things that we must do for the things that we want to do? Well, I'll tell you what happens: The things that we want to do slowly go away because pretty soon we're only left with the things that we have to do. When you learn to demonstrate urgency for things that are truly urgent, you will create a great habit of doing those things that must be done as quickly and as efficiently as possible. In addition, you'll create opportunities to do other things with more flexibility.

RULE 2.16: Create Value With Your Words

When I was young, I always thought my father spoke everything in hyperbole. Every lesson that he taught or every example he gave always seemed to be so extreme to me – now that I'm a man, I clearly understand his methods. For instance, he would always say that a man should be able to live or die by his word. And I never really gave that much thought, until I start dealing with people. People whose words don't have much value. People who will say that they will do something, and partially do it, or sometimes do it, or do it but not within the parameters of what was agreed. "I'll be there at 5:00" and they show up at 5:40. "I will fulfill this obligation" but they don't, or they partially do it, or they have some varied range of excuses as to why they were unsuccessful.

When you develop a brand that involves integrity in your words (RULE 2.2), people know that you are going to deliver on your promises day in and day out, then your words become valuable, your words become currency. You are able to create opportunities with your words because of the behavior that is attached to it. So, make sure that what you say you're going to do you do, and those things you say you're not going to do, you don't. And when you say you're going to do something, do it exactly how you said you would do it, or better. The value that you can create with your words will become a credit line for you in the future.

RULE 2.17: Be Ordinary First

Mentoring is one of the most energizing activities that I'm involved in. Listening to people talk about their ambitions, their goals and dreams, really excites me. There are so many people that have extraordinary ideas that could positively impact so many people in the community, the world even. But the question is, what stops people from becoming extraordinary? What stops people from developing these super ideas and powerful enterprises?

Well, I'll tell you what I've seen – simply put, the inability to be ordinary first. In essence, before you can be Superman, you simply have to be a man. Likewise, before you can be an extraordinary person you have to be able to master being an ordinary person. How do you do that?

Well, you be consistent in doing what ordinary people do. You meet and exceed the standards that ordinary people are expected to meet in life whether it's work, hobby or play. If that means demonstrating an ability to keep your word and execute your commitments, then you do that, not one time, but consistently. If that means that you are required to be to work at 8:00 on a daily basis, then you do that – not 8:30 because of traffic, but 8:00. If that means that you need to have a bank account, and automobile, or any of the range of things that ordinary people do or have, you need to develop the capacity to do that before you can be more than that.

The fact is, if you attempt to do more than the basics, you are overshooting, trying to be Superman before you've mastered being an ordinary man. There will be a time that the basics will be required and you won't have a demonstrated capacity to do the ordinary things with any consistency. Remember, consistency in doing "Man" things is what will separate the men from the boys.

RULE 2.18: Recognize Your Proclivities

I have habits and tendencies. Some good, and some that I'm not as proud of. We all do. What's more, some of our tendencies and habits become exposed when we're under stress. It is said that stress brings out our character. I liken this to a pot of cold soup on the stove. You look at the pot and you see a murky mix of broth. But turn up the heat and stand by – shortly the soup begins to boil and everything that it's in that soup will soon rise to the top. It is the same with men. Not only will pressure and stress reveal our character traits, but our tendencies and habits will also be put on display when we react to various stimuli.

We need to take it upon ourselves to be better acquainted with these proclivities. Why? Because everyone else sees your proclivities. If everyone around you has seen film on you, and they understand how you're likely to react under certain circumstances, then who has the advantage? If everyone but you knows how you will respond under particular circumstances, then you lose your ability to manage yourself, and your environment. You are now more susceptible to being used, controlled and manipulated.

RULE 2.19: Denial is Venom

So we all have tendencies and habits that can create hurdles for us ... or do we?

In my experiences with mentoring and coaching, I've found that self-awareness, or the lack thereof, is one of the greatest challenges in the development of men.

We think we have what we don't, and we refuse to recognize what we have that we don't need. When we deny what's obvious to anyone that's looking, we are only hurting ourselves. Moreover, this denial becomes the venom that will slowly degrade our ability to advance past certain challenges, crises that will persist because of our inability to address the very issues that we deny having.

RULE 2.20: Be an Advocate for Yourself

If you live long enough you're going to develop an audience. And your audience will not necessarily be fans, or friendly. If you're doing well, you'll have critics. If you're doing poorly, you'll have critics. It is important that you understand what you have to offer, as well as what you have already offered. Sometimes they aren't equal. But in any case, you must develop the ability to speak in support of yourself. Not in a spirit of arrogance or defiance, but as an advocate. Always avoid the opportunity to pile on or be overly critical of yourself. There will always be a long line of other people willing to do that for you.

RULE 2.21: Develop a Proactive Mindset

If you know where you don't want to go, what you don't want to eat, who you don't want to be like, what you don't want to try, and you don't do any of those things, what have you accomplished? Conversely, if you have a destination in mind, know some things that you are willing to try, have someone in your life that you like to emulate, and you successfully do just one of those things, what have you accomplished?

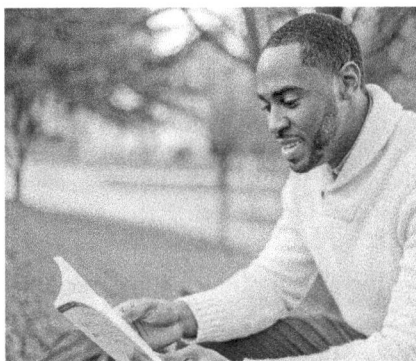

Well, who's to say, but what we do know is that you have moved from where you were, you have made progress, you have grown, and you have done something.

The fact is, when you develop a proactive mindset you live with a spirit of accomplishment. You are always working to move forward in your quest to accomplish something. The alternative is being reactive, or just stagnant. Knowing nothing but what you don't want. Or spending your time dealing with circumstances that spring up. Created opportunities come from knowing and doing.

RULE 2.22: Be Self-aware and Self-accountable

You'd be surprised how many people have great ideas, the time and the resources to be successful. They even have a detailed plan that they work on implementing on a daily basis. But still, success seems to never be within reach. They spend great amounts of time updating and adjusting business, marketing, and personal development plans, but never can seem to get the traction needed to develop momentum. Why is this? Well, in many cases it's due to a poorly calibrated sense of self-awareness. You see, you can have a great idea and a great plan, but if you don't have the tools or you don't accurately measure the resources that you have to accomplish the task, you're always going to be struggling to reach your destination.

Consider this: You have a ticket on Flight 32 nonstop from Washington to Los Angeles. You're waiting at the gate, but there is no plane. People come, and people go, but they never put your flight on the board. Eventually you go to the ticket counter and express concern and the gate agent says, "Sir, this ticket that you have is from Washington to Los Angeles." And you say, "Yes of course, I know this. Where's the plane leaving from?" And she replies, "The plane is leaving from Washington. But sir, we are in Philadelphia!"

I love this example (also used to make a point in the beginning of Part Two), because it speaks to self-awareness, or the lack thereof in the most basic of senses. How many times do we create plans that lead us from a spot that we don't even feel is right, or from a completely wrong location? Yet time and time again we'll say our path leaves from point B to point C, except we're not at point B yet. So any work that we do along this plan is going to be flawed. We may have some successes along the way, but those successes are haphazard and often come along by chance. We will not be able to be systematic in our approach or develop sustainable momentum towards our goals until we know where we are. But sometimes we can't figure that out by ourselves. That's why having a good mentor is especially important.

When we find out where we are, who we are, and what we have to work with, then it is incumbent upon each of us to hold ourselves accountable to what we have to do to grow. We must grow what we have, from where we actually are, to further develop, and move to where we want to be.

RULE 2.23: Don't Marry Yourself to Being Right

Right is relative. As a man, there's tremendously more value in getting the right answer – and gathering the right information – than there is being right. Circumstances will arise where you'll have all the information available to you, and still not have the right answer. And because you had all the information (or so you thought) from your perspective you were convinced that you made the right decision. The right decision, however, does not always translate into the right answer.

Don't be so concerned with being right. Be more concerned about arriving at the right answer. Sometimes that may involve someone else having the vital information or better perspective. On occasion, simply recognizing that someone else's perspective is better than yours will expose you to additional information that will allow you to see a more complete landscape. The more information that you have from the broadest possible perspectives will enhance your ability to make decisions that will present you with the right outcomes. So, be more concerned about getting the answer than being right.

RULE 2.24: Recognize and Resist the Man Killers

In the beginning of this book we defined the characteristics that make a man. And just like a thing can be made, it can be destroyed. One thing every man must avoid, or overcome, are the "man killers". Jealousy, possessiveness, laziness and insecurity have killed more men than all the bullets, disease and pestilence since the beginning of time.

When you open yourself up to jealousy, you become so concerned about what other people have, or have accomplished, that you lose sight of your own ability to produce.

Moreover, an unhealthy concern about possessing things (and in some cases people), will diminish your ability to grow and gain more things. A closed hand can accept no gifts.

Laziness is one of the worst killers. A man that does nothing achieves nothing.

And last but certainly not least, is insecurity. A man that constantly needs other people to bolster his ego or confidence, cannot sustain the characteristics that make a man a man. Insecurities, jealousy, laziness and possessiveness are characteristics that are self-preserving and self-feeding. These are dangerous because they can survive and thrive without any reinforcement. They have to be killed dead by crowding them out with activity of the positive, and opposite nature.

RULE 2.25: Develop Sustainable Habits for Growth

In my life, I've had many discussions on self-improvement, career development and personal growth. I've talked to people that have overcome substantial addictions and debilitating habits. And while a great amount of time has been shared talking about methods to avoid bad habits and toxic tendencies, not enough time is given to the "how to's" of developing good habits. As with developing a proactive mindset (RULE 2.21), it is just as important to not focus on what you need to stop doing, as it is to tune in to what you can and should be doing.

We have a finite number of hours in a day. Sometimes it's simply a matter of crowding the bad things out with the good. Creating enough positive, sustainable habits will inevitably reduce the amount of time that you have to be involved in things that are going to subtract from your life. Now the key here is sustainable habits for growth. It's not enough to develop a habit as it is to be able to sustain it.

Take my gym experience. I tell myself that I've got to stay in shape, I've got to be more physically active. So, I go to the gym. I've even brainwashed myself enough to believe that if I go seven to ten days in a row it'll become a positive habit for me.

So, I start out hard on day one of the workout. Of course, the soreness starts to set in but I push through. Before you know it, workout days five and six blow by, and now I'm really feeling good about myself. I now have a habit, and I'm mentally set on going to the gym at least five consecutive days every week. So time goes by and around day nine, life starts to happen. I have a late meeting, or an appointment, or I'm just worn out. I miss a day, but no problem. I'll just go tomorrow. Tomorrow is fine, but then I miss the next day. And then I miss the next two days. Now, I'm unable to get back into the gym state of mind. Before I know it, I've missed five days in a row.

This is the point that I usually start feeling frustrated and defeated.

It took me the longest time to realize that I was setting myself up for disappointment by having such aggressive expectations, considering my work and family obligations. What I came to realize is that I had to set sustainable goals. I needed to create sustainable habits. Now, instead of having a goal to be in the gym five consecutive days per week, my expectations are to simply have an aggressive workout five days per week. This means if I cannot go to the gym, then I'll get on the stationary bike, or treadmill, at home. By making this small adjustment, my habits are now much more sustainable than they were before, and I'm feeling better about my opportunities to meet my goals.

RULE 2.26: Set Goals, Not Dreams

I said before that dreams are free (RULE 2.7), so no one has an excuse for not having one. That being said, it is vitally important that you are clear on the differences between your goals and your dreams. Though it sounds simple, many people confuse the two.

Here's a tip: Dreams are thought on, goals are acted upon. You can have a dream without doing anything. In fact, some dreams come to us in our sleep. Other dreams come to us while we meditate or sit idly away. Dreams are those things that we wish we could achieve in a world where circumstances are perfect. Usually these dreams are nebulous in description and content. Dreams rarely have precise definition.

Goals, on the other hand, are those things that we act upon in a sequence of steps that should take us to – or at least closer to – a finite place or outcome. When we conflate the two we set ourselves up for disappointment. Before you can treat a dream like a goal, you have to move it into the realm of attainment. This can be done only when you accumulate the appropriate resources for this to happen. This is a vital step in separating, or transforming, dreams from goals. Now you can move forward.

RULE 2.27: Status Can't Be Your Driver

Generally speaking, what drives you? Do you know?

The fact is, people are driven by different stimuli. We all have different motivations for what we do in life. The jobs we work, the cars we drive, the social circles that we participate in. Everything we do has a driver.

It's important to know what your motivations are, because those things will ultimately become your master. Do not allow a desire for status or attention to be your driver. If you do, it will take you to places that you don't always want to go.

Status can be an intoxicating thing to some people. And for others, the need for the attention that status brings, can be as addictive as drugs. The problem with allowing status to be your driver is that this need has an insatiable appetite. You can never do enough to have the status that you want, or think that you deserve. Everything that you accomplish that brings you status, or gets you recognized, is fleeting. It's like a flash. It's here, then gone, which leaves you looking for the next opportunity to be recognized, or relevant again.

This lifestyle can be exhausting and force you to compromise some things that are valuable to you. The worst part of allowing status to be your driver, is when you get tired of doing what has to be done to maintain it, more times than not, there is still a requirement for you to continue to do more. The status monster must be fed continually – once you create it, you must feed it, or be consumed by it.

RULE 2.28: Fear of Failure is Emotional Paralysis

From time to time I get involved in coaching and mentoring opportunities. I love to see the energy and the desire in the eyes of so many. It also makes me feel a sense of pride and value by being able to offer information and advice that can further inspire people to achieve. That being said, I often ask mentees about their dreams and their backgrounds, and they tend to offer up a bunch of information and qualifications.

Then, I'll ask them what's holding them back. What's slowing their progress in accomplishing their goals? And here's what happens: I'll hear things like ...

- "Well, I'm waiting on the right time."

- "I'm not where I need to be financially."

- "I'm trying to check some boxes."

- "I just don't have the time."

- "I got too many bills or financial responsibilities to take that risk right now."

- "I'm working on it a little bit at a time, on the side."

I get any range of responses, all virtually the same. Everybody is looking for a nice, comfortable transition into what they want to do, because they are afraid of failing. They are so frightened at the thought of what may happen if things don't go the way they need to go, that they plan and research themselves to death. Not execute, but plan.

In rare cases people will just say, "I'm afraid I won't be successful," to which my response is, "How many times have you gotten up in the morning, on your way to work, and said to yourself, 'I hope I'm successful.' Or how many times have you laid in bed, afraid to get up and go to work because you were concerned about whether you'd be successful or not?" To date, I've had very few to confirm that to be the case. And the reason why is because when you go to work for somebody, success is required. It is the expectation of the job, whatever the job is. You're required to come to work and do a job and meet certain standards and expectations.

So, if you're able to do as much for somebody else, what's stopping you from doing the same for yourself? The best way not to fail is to make sure that failure is not an option. To be clear, when I say "failure is not an option," I'm not saying you won't ever miss your goal or fall short. I am saying that the overall outcome of your work will not account for failure. You must be successful!

In essence, failures are a part of the process in the short run. You fail, then recalibrate, then you succeed. However, if you fail and don't ever try again, then that's absolute failure. Absolute failure cannot be an option.

If you don't do a thing because you are afraid that you won't be successful, you'll never move. You'll be paralyzed. So, understand that a fear of failure is emotional paralysis.

RULE 2.29: You Can't Become a "True Man" Overnight

What man doesn't want to be considered the head of his household, or thought of as the leader, or chief provider for his family?

I ask this question because there are quite a few households where, for whatever reason, the man has relegated himself to being just one tier above the kids, when it comes to defining his place or authority in the household.

What I mean is that, in too many cases, women have been forced to take on so many core responsibilities in the household, that they naturally assume the leadership and authority roles of chief provider and head of the family.

As I've said in the past, in the absence of a man, women will attempt to morph into that role to manage those responsibilities. But what about those households, or relationships, where a man is indeed present, with all of his faculties, but still has to defer to the leadership presence of the woman?

Well, this is simple. More times than not, he has failed to walk in, or fulfill his role in the family. But let's hit the brakes right here for a second. Before we go any further, I think it's important for us to understand that while the economic contribution to the family is essential, a man's ability to provide, protect, and preserve extends well beyond the reach of his paycheck. I say that, to say this: You are not less of a man because your woman makes more money than you. Your responsibilities to your household and family are far greater than that. If anything, you are less of a man when you fail to do what is necessary to consistently fulfill your leadership responsibilities.

Now, to circle back to our previous conversation, if a household has a healthy man present, but the woman is assuming the leadership, and authoritative roles, it is generally because the man in the house does not meet her expectation for what a man is. And though there are many reasons for this, they all dead-end at the same point. If your woman doesn't recognize you as a "true man" today, she won't tomorrow either. This means that you've got a lot of work to do, and fast.

Take Karl, for example ...

In an open discussion, he expressed his frustration about having to constantly verbally joust with his wife, when it came to making key decisions in the house. As you probably suspect, there is a back story.

Karl actually met his wife Leisa in the mist of being unemployed. And at that time, she was the best thing in the world for him. She was super supportive and understanding, constantly motivating him to push forward in the job search. Their chemistry was great. So much so, that they fell in love, moved-in together and had a baby. A short time after the baby's birth, the two got married.

In the midst of all of the change they had experienced in their relationship, one thing remained constant – Karl's inability to become gainfully employed. This led to him falling deeper into a slump. His daily routine included dropping Leisa off at work, in her car. Then he drove around looking for job opportunities for the balance of the morning. He'd then go home to find himself later watching soap operas and playing video games until the time came to pick up the baby from daycare, and later, the wife from work.

One week of this activity led to the next, and while Leisa remained loving and supportive, she found herself working even harder to be able to provide the things necessary to sustain them. Eventually her support eroded into frustration, which more and more frequently, turned into confrontation. Following one confrontation too many, Leisa issued an ultimatum.

"Get a decent job, or get another family."

Sadly, things had to devolve to such a level before Karl could summon enough follow-through to secure a really good job.

Now fast forward three months to present day, and we find that Karl is taking on more and more responsibility for managing the household, financially and otherwise. And while Leisa is eager to off-load some of those taxing responsibilities, she is not interested in relinquishing any leadership authority. Her failure to do so has Karl feeling frustrated and confused.

The key to learning for this rule is this: When you fail to fulfill your role as a man, a woman will attempt to fill the void the best way that she can. Even when you decide to start doing those things that you should have been doing in the past, you cannot expect her to immediately relinquish that authority and give it to you. You must simply do, and do, and do more, of what you're supposed to do as a man on a consistent basis, and allow your behavior and leadership to create an environment that makes her feel more comfortable submitting in certain areas of the relationship.

RULE 2.30: Know Your Limits Then Push Them

An important aspect of manhood is growing and thriving. You can't expect to grow and develop without first knowing your limits, and then pushing them. When you consider birds in nature, they were first chicks inside an eggshell. That shell was a safe, warm home to them for months. But what if they never recognized their limit and therefore never pushed them? They would soon die from malnutrition. Instead, healthy chicks innately know their limits and automatically know to push those limits, chipping away more and more at the inside of their shells until the shell breaks and they make their way out. What's more, to continue with this analogy, these young birds understand that they must one day leave the safety and security of their nests. Only then can they learn to fly and take off on their own.

Same for us. It is essential that we live with a spirit of self-growth and development. You must be introspective and you must identify the tangible and intangible barriers that serve as your limits, whatever your limits may be. Perhaps your limits are some low-level phobia of some sort, such as a fear of commitment, a fear of failure, what have you. Your limits may include the inability to handle your finances responsibly. Whatever the limits, they always include a whole range of things that limit your ability and vision.

As a man, it's important to constantly self-evaluate to know where your opportunities for personal growth lie. Only then are you able to meet those limitations head-on and actively work to move beyond them in your quest for personal growth.

RULE 2.31: Frame Your Own Success

What exactly is success? Well simply put, it's the act of accomplishing your aim or objective. Of importance is to note that you must have an aim or objective to reach, prior to attempting to frame your success.

Not long ago, I was attending a weekend car meet where I was approached by a gentleman that I grew up with. Keep in mind that I haven't seen, or communicated with him in over 20 years, but that fact did not stop him from asking me a range of invasive questions. So you'll understand why I was taken aback, shocked, amazed – even surprised – when out of the blue he starts asking me bizarre questions like:

- "How much money do you make?"

- "What's your hustle?"

- "What do you do for a living?"

- "How can you afford a car like that?"

With a frustrated pitch, he began a tirade claiming that he works harder than I do, but he can't buy a ride like mine. He even went so far as to say that he lost his woman to a man that had a ride like mine. I did not have the heart to tell him that I was the man, but that's neither here nor there. The point is that this man was incensed at the thought that he is struggling, but I appear to be doing well.

I'm in the car, sitting up, speechless. I felt as though I was in some bizarre parallel universe where perfect strangers come up to you, and out of the blue, start interrogating you about the validity of your success. No, not likely. The real question is what would drive a guy to do such a thing? What level of insecurity does a man need to have to be fighting mad at the thought of one of his peers attaining something that he has failed to do?

At this point, I try to blow him off in the most respectful way I can. I tell him, "I don't know what you do, and I don't know what you call success. All I can tell you is that I get up and work hard every day."

As gently as I try to handle the conversation the madder he gets. He responds back, with an elevated tone, "Hey man look, I work hard every day too. I bet I work harder than you. I work 50-60 hours a week in that hot-ass plant screwing those widgets in those sockets."

"Look, I don't know what it is you're doing," I said. "I don't know how long you do it. I don't know how much money you make, or what your circumstances are that keep you from where you want to be. All I can tell you is, I do what I do, and you should do what you do, or do something different to get you to where you want to be."

The learning is this: You can't be successful in reaching your goals doing what someone else is doing. You can only be successful doing what you should be doing. Set your own goal, build the necessary plans, then execute.

RULE 2.32: Know the Givers and Takers

In your lifetime, you'll develop a range of relationships with a countless number of people that can ultimately be divided into two categories. I like to call these people givers and takers, people who add to your life, and people who take away from your life.

We all have givers and takers in our lives in many different areas. Whether in finances, emotional health, personal or professional growth, it is essential that we become comfortable identifying the people that are contributing to our lives more so than taking away. Regardless of the person or area of life that they affect, you have to know the value of their impact and why. Only then can you determine the level of participation you allow them to have in your life.

The challenge in determining if someone is a giver or a taker lies in being able to evaluate them and their role in your life over time. Moreover, you must understand that a person's role may mean that they take consistently in one area but give more consistently in another. So, the overall value contribution of that person to your life is what determines if they are a giver or a taker.

RULE 2.33: Overcoming the Survival Mindset

Life is about living, not surviving.

One of the greatest factors that impact the quality of the man is the mindset that he has in approaching life – more specifically a mindset centered on living, instead of surviving. Too many of us, too often, become prisoners of the survival mindset. This mindset sets the stage for us to do all that we can, to end up with "just enough" to survive the day, week or pay cycle. It opens us up to a steady flow of want, frustration, physical and emotional fatigue. Whether financially or emotionally, in many cases, the survival mindset often causes us to continue to make poor judgment decisions because of our needs and desires to have things or people that we aren't financially, or emotionally able to afford. In other cases, a lack of vision keeps us bound to the same regimens that yield the same results.

Conversely, the living mindset is one of exploration and exposure, creating opportunities to enjoy greater and greater experiences in life. This mindset helps to create an environment for you to accumulate more physical and emotional assets. Excess instead of just enough. With excess we can do more than survive the week. We can now plan on doing more and being greater, a result of now having resources and inspiration.

RULE 2.34: Just Say HELP

In the course of writing this book, one of the things that I wanted to spend a significant amount of time emphasizing is the importance of having vision, and being able to build pathways that will allow us, as men, to move from where we are, to that vision.

Success, goal attainment, and personal development are all tremendous benchmarks. But as I think and reflect on where I am at this very moment, I would be remiss if I did not speak to the importance of being able to say one four-letter word: HELP!

In my life, I've been fortunate to be flanked by a bunch of strong men. Not just my father and grandfather. But uncles, cousins and other people that were in proximity to me as I was growing up, who were excellent examples of men striving, men producing, and men taking care of families. That being said, one of the things that I found lacking in my development as a man, even in my experience as a father, is the importance of communicating that it is okay to need help.

I think sometimes as men, we equate a need for help with a sense of weakness. We see vulnerability as an opportunity to be taken advantage of, or looked down upon. And while I will always stay true to my belief that a man must be independent, project strength and leadership, I will also say that a man's strength, at least in part, comes from an ability to know when he needs help.

I remember working on my 8th-grade science project. It was on the Space Shuttle Columbia. The project consisted of a detailed report on the space shuttle, an in-depth diagram on a backdrop, and a plastic scale model of the spacecraft. I had worked diligently on this project. I had assembled my presentation, fixed my poster board, colored my drawings, and assembled my model. Everything was done in great detail, and I felt confident that I would get a gold medal. There was one last thing to be done. I needed to paint the plastic model, and add the decals. I was going for as much authenticity as possible. I wasn't much on painting (in fact I had zero experience at it), so I asked my father to help me.

"NOPE! I'll have no part in it."

I stood there with a lost look on my face wondering why. He went on to say, "Son, let this be a lesson to you. Never put anybody in a situation, or a position, where they can come back and say they helped."

This is but one example of the types of man-framing conversations that I experienced over my life. If I had this conversation once, I promise you, I've had hundreds like it from my father and grandfather, all expressing the importance of individuality, as well as independence. And while I understood the spirit of what my dad was saying, his messaging over the years left me with a mental disposition of never wanting to seek help from anyone. Not Mom, not girlfriend, not best friend, no one. The worst part of this mindset is that asking for help became a foreign feeling, a bad feeling. Needing to ask someone to help me out of a situation was something I was absolutely ashamed to do. This has led me to some very dark places in my life. Not knowing how to ask for help, or being ashamed to even need help, has caused me to endure emotional experiences that were absolutely unnecessary, and unrelenting. As a result, I've sought confidence in people that I had no business even looking to. I also found myself filtering out people that cared about me. Sadly, my inability to know how to ask for help has fueled my poor judgment, simply because I was compelled to display strength over vulnerability.

PART THREE

WALK LIKE A MAN

Men – "true men" – are known just as much by what they do, as they are by what they don't do. As men, we tend to be "pack-minded." We generally enjoy congregating among ourselves, jousting to establish various "pecking orders," as well as admiring and emulating the behaviors of each other. With this "pack-minded" behavior, we have tremendous opportunities to challenge each other to be more than we are on virtually every level.

Part Three of *Mannishlaws* speaks to the tenets of smart living. Using a greater concentration of real stories, I hope to share some examples that, as bizarre as some may seem, are things that men deal with, and should learn from. My hope is that we can extract some type of basic learnings from these events that may help us with our judgement during our continued growth in manhood.

RULE 3.1: A "True Man" Can't be Held Emotionally Hostage

In RULE 2.6, we mentioned the importance of having an outwardly recognizable belief system as well as self-regulated standards. When we become emotionally involved with people (and things to a lesser degree), we can find ourselves in situations where compromising our beliefs seems to be the easiest way out of a problem. The greater the potential for loss, the more willing we can be in flexing out of character, or standards, to protect what we have. Personally, over the years, I've been caught in a few circumstances where I was willing to pay God, and the devil both, to keep certain people from knowing about my antics. But what I've learned is that it is much better to accept responsibility for a behavior, than it is to be held hostage buy it.

This takes me to the story of Jim.

Jim had experienced a stretch of hard luck over the past year or so. He was struggling to recover from substance abuse, and the toll it had taken on his family. He was also working hard with his wife to hold the marriage together, as he had been caught in an affair with the choir director at church. All of these issues were working in concert to make Jim's life utterly miserable. Every day he found himself walking on "eggshells" with his wife, trying his very best not to do anything that would look questionable or remind her of his transgressions. Something as simple as saying, "Honey, I'm headed to the store, do you need anything?" could easily be met with a response of, "What do you need from the store? I know you're just trying to get out, so you can call that B@#$% from the church. How about I go to the store with you?"

Dealing with this type of challenge, while in recovery, was a struggle, on top of a struggle. So, I could understand why he was so panicked when he reached out to me asking for advice.

Jim said that a friend of his wife shared a video with him that she had recorded on her smartphone a few days earlier. The video footage was of him sloppy drunk in the casino, kissing and groping on an unidentified woman, a woman who appeared to be a willing participant. Now, here's the rub: The friend of the wife (owner of the video) was willing to destroy the video for a $2,000 cash payment, and some private time with Jim. What was Jim to do?

Well, we talked it over, and eventually we reached a point where he found value in coming clean with his wife.

Jim chose to have the difficult conversation. Now, as passionate as he was in admitting his mistakes, and empathizing with her pain, he also chose to be firm in declaring that he would no longer deal with the daily reminders of his past transgressions.

Sadly, as contrite and empathetic as he was, his requirement for his wife to cease with the daily doses of "failure reminders" was more than she was willing to go along with.

Jim's marriage ended, but so did the daily misery and stress associated with it. He's doing so much better now. Looking good, sounding good, and moving forward with an air of confidence.

Look, I'd never advocate the destruction of a marriage, or relationship in general. Well, except for in the cases where the marriage itself is destructive. But in some cases, the death of a relationship is a necessary step in the progression to good emotional health. Here's what you have to realize (I shared this with Jim): Life is going to produce countless opportunities for us to trip, slip, and fall according to our vices. It could be liquor, it could be women, it could be money. Whatever your weakness is, rest assured life will be there dangling the bait. So when you fall – and you will fall – you need to know that there's going to be an audience there to witness it. But you can't be afraid of that. You've got to be just as bold in owning your fall, as you were when you took the bait.

Only then can you begin to break free of the bondage associated with the transgressions of your past.

RULE 3.2: Deadbeat Dads

Anyone that knows me well will tell you that I have strong opinions on the role of fatherhood. All throughout this book I harp on the importance and value of men growing and developing in manhood. That being said, nothing is more important in manhood than actively fulfilling the responsibility of fatherhood. All men should understand that the role of a father cannot be substituted or replaced. What we do, or fail to do as fathers, has a rippling effect that impacts generations to come. So, when we take the role of "Absentee Dad," "Sperm Donor" or simply pretend that we don't know that we have a responsibility to participate in raising a child, we put additional pressure on someone else to do the job that we originally committed to doing, by words or actions.

Think of it this way: You and I decide to rob a bank. I'll drive the getaway car, and you'll go in and hold them up. Except that when you come out of the bank with all the money, I'm gone. I'm nowhere to be found in the getaway car, which means you're standing there holding the bag, later trying your best to explain to the judge how it all was just a big mistake. As a result, you've got 15-30 years hard time to serve. Why? Because this wasn't your first offense. You've had priors. You have a demonstrated history of poor judgement.

Now let's apply this to the term we disparagingly call "Deadbeat Dad." You know, that guy that establishes enough of a relationship with a woman to get her pregnant, then disappears (or hangs around to leech), nowhere to be found for the financial support, growth and personal protection of that kid. As a result, the mom and child do 18 to 20 years of hard time, dealing with various life crisis, ups and downs.

And while I personally believe that "Deadbeat Dads" are some of the worse human beings ever made, that's only half the story. The guy may have just turned out to be a "Deadbeat Dad," but he was a deadbeat all along. Why didn't the woman know that? She could have known, and in fact she should have known, before she amended his "Deadbeat" title with "Dad."

In many of these "Deadbeat Dad" cases, if women are honest with themselves, they'll admit that the "Deadbeat Dad" wasn't doing much, or offering much value to the relationship pre-child, and yet they were still involved with the men on a level that was deep enough to make a baby. So, in essence, she helped plan the heist (referring to the example above). Which means the time she gets is well deserved. The problem is the time and struggle experienced by the mother and child, in the absence of that father, adversely affects their views and expectations of life and men.

As men we must take pause before flirting with the opportunity, or risk, of creating life. With that comes responsibilities that long outlast the initial pleasure. But if you are a father, you must embrace the task. Your child deserves your involvement in their life. Even if you realize that you are the "Deadbeat Dad" that I'm speaking of, it's not too late to become involved. But understand, nothing about fatherhood is easy. Enjoyable, yes; easy, no!

RULE 3.3: Life is About More Than Stuff

We live in an ultra-materialistic time. A time where more, and more people are finding themselves struggling to acquire more, and more things that have minimal overall impact on their stability of home, health, or overall quality of life. People are killing themselves to get "stuff!" For what?

And what's more is, the latest and greatest "stuff," is always about to be launched. People will proudly wait in line for hours to get the newest smartphone, even when the newest phone is virtually indistinguishable from the one they already have. I have personally known people that have bought cars, only to trade them in on the latest model 18 months later, regardless of the loss. We are in a time where people are becoming "stuff broke."

Consider my friend Josef. He and I often meet for lunch just to small talk, and stay current with each other, and any necessary gossip. But one day Josef was visibly worried, and being the concerned friend, I lent an ear.

He was in a bad place, financially, and I felt bad for him.

He goes on to tell me that he's paying about $3,000 a month in mortgage, about $2,200 in revolving credit card debt, he's got two late-model cars for which he's paying about $2,100 monthly. Put that on top of two kids in private school and one in the second semester of college. He's cash-strapped and ready to end it all. Then sprinkle in the fact that his wife is stressing him pretty hard because they hadn't had a vacation in about seven months. Her friends are going out of the country on lavish trips, while she can only go to the pool at the country club.

He asks me to give him a little direction, because he doesn't know where to turn, and can't even think clearly.

I tell him, "You're in a bad spot. You are 'stuff broke.'"

"Stuff broke?"

"Yeah, stuff broke. You got all this stuff and you can't even live. All your resources have been tied up in accumulating stuff. And the worst part of it is, all of the stuff that you have isn't even worth what you owe on it. It's a bad place to be."

Being "stuff broke" is a problem a lot of us have. We spend so much time developing fictitious projections of who we are, that all we can do is live for what people think of us. Sometimes it may even get to the point, like with this brother, where we can't even appreciate life.

Life is about living, not surviving (see RULE 2.33), but you can't live if every dollar you make is committed to something before it even hits your bank account.

Now, let me be clear, there's nothing wrong with stuff; stuff can be good.

It's good to look good. It's great to feel good about the stuff you have. It's great to get compliments about your car, your house, the parties you have. But if it's all about stuff, what happens when the stuff is gone?

For a man, life has got to be about more than just stuff. Your net worth is based on more than stuff.

RULE 3.4: Align Your Expectations and Goals

I believe that every man and woman has the right – the obligation even – to be successful and to enjoy life on as many levels as possible. But, our expectations must be in line with the goals we set. Simply said, we can't work hard planting peaches, and expect for apples to grow. This rule brings to mind an old relationship that I found myself being asked out of.

One day, my then-girlfriend came to me and told me she had the roadmap to success and prosperity, and it didn't necessarily include me. Hearing this, I was shocked and disappointed. But I was more curious than anything.

"You've got a roadmap to success – what's your plan?" I asked. "What are you trying to accomplish?"

"I'm going to have a multi-million-dollar business," she said. "I'm going to have a lot of assets. I'm going to do a lot of traveling, and just enjoy life. The first thing I'm going to do is get back in school."

At this point, I told her I understood, and that I was sorry I couldn't be part of that process. But I asked, "Where are you going to school? UCLA, University of Alabama, Georgia Tech?"

She stopped, looked at me and said, "Heck no, I'm not going to any of those places. I'm going to nail school."

I just thought, "Nail school?" I was at a loss for words. Far be it for me to tell anybody what to do with their future, or how to frame their success, but what I will stress is that you have to keep your expectations in line with your actions.

This is one personal example, but I could share many other instances where I've observed people set goals that, if they accomplish, will not offer the anticipated return. As men with limited resources, we must become good at setting goals and building plans, and even better at anticipating outcomes to our actions. When we become better in this area, we make major strides in becoming able to create greater opportunities for ourselves.

RULE 3.5: Don't Get Caught Up in a Bundle

Some say you are better served in taking the path of least resistance. I actually prefer the path of no resistance. I'm a pretty reasonable guy. I've been known to go along with some pretty far-fetched things, simply because they ultimately made sense. But there is a new bundling phenomenon (as seen with cable being bundled with Internet and phone) that I'm seeing lately that's getting to be absolutely absurd. I mean, do not make me buy something I don't want, because you put it with something else that you know I need. If I want to pay $49 for Internet, then let me pay that. Don't tell me I can get Internet for $19 if I buy the cable and the telephone. With that, I'm paying $150 instead of $49 for the Internet. And still, while I'm paying $150, you're telling me I'm saving $300 per month on the total package. The problem is I never wanted the package. I just wanted the Internet!

I mention this particular bundling example because I've started to observe similar tactics being demonstrated in relationships. Here's what I mean:

I'm having a conversation at dinner and the woman tells me, "Baby, you make me feel like I've never felt before. You're my sun, my moon, my stars. My whole world revolves around you – I never felt this way." I'm sitting up, thinking "Wow, I wasn't expecting to hear that. I just asked you to pass the salt." But she was sitting up, gazing at me, looking into my soul. She goes on to say, "Because I feel this way, and I never felt this way before, I'm going to give you all of my soul and all of my affection." So I knew I had to respond with something.

I look at her and say, "Baby, look, there are some things that I've never experienced, that I've experienced with you. It's a great relationship. I'm really loving the way things are going. And you know what, I'll meet you there – I'm going to give you all my love and all of my affection as well."

She looks at me and says, "And?"

I'm looking at her and I say, "And what?"

"You're going to give me your love and your affection," she says. "I get that. And what else?"

I respond, "Well what else is there?"

"Look honey, you've got to bundle this thing. You've got to give me your love, your affection, and some declarations, like trips, like handbags, money – a lot of stuff. You've got to bundle it."

She was trying to tell me that if I bundled it, you get a better value. My thought: "Really?"

Wrong!

So this is a good time for me to say that I did not fault her for expressing her expectations. For any relationship to prosper, each person has to know what the other person wants, needs, and is willing to do for the relationship. My fault with her was that I expressed what I was willing to give, and she set the requirement far beyond what I offered.

The bottom line is this: You can't get caught up in a bundle, because you're going to end up spending more time, money and emotional capital than you originally planned for.

RULE 3.6: You Must Set Boundaries for Your Friends

As men, we generally do what we like. We get together in groups at events and discuss man stuff. We may look at the women who go by and make a few wishes. But there's usually nothing more than a bunch of lies being told, and a lot of laughter being had. The problems tend to happen when we men begin to violate unwritten rules or socially accepted boundaries.

Picture this: I was with my crew. We were standing around smoking stogies, laughing and such. My ol' lady walked up, and my friend Jessup (is what we'll call him) said, "Hey girl, come over here and give me a hug. I've not seen you in forever."

I said, "Dude, hold on! You haven't seen her in forever, and 'give me a hug' – there won't be any hugging going on, considering the type of conversation we just had about all these other women walking by."

"What are you talking about? We're cool," he said.

"Yeah, we're cool ... cool enough to have conversations about these other women, but bro, we're not cool enough for you to be putting your hands on my woman. In fact, there is no scenario, whatsoever, where you're putting your hands on her. Short of her choking, and you're trying to clear her air passageway. Better yet, let her choke. It'll be a good lesson to her, to chew her food better."

The point is this: Sometimes friends will see the social behavior boundaries as blurred, or even non-existent. It's in these cases that we must be comfortable setting clear and firm boundaries with them. Otherwise they're not going to be friends for long.

RULE 3.7: You Can't Kick It With Coworkers

Who among us hasn't cut out of work early and hit the "Happy Hour" scene with our co-workers a time or two? I've certainly been guilty of it. But what I've learned is that we've got to put this workplace social hour junk to an end – you can't do it. Healthy working relationships with coworkers are essential for success in our professional lives. Sometimes social interactions outside of work can help enhance our relationships at work. But be careful. This rule explains why "You can't kick it with your co-workers."

I remember agreeing to do a "Happy Hour" event with some co-workers one day after work. We were having a great time, good conversation, cheap drinks – or maybe it's cheap conversation and good drinks. Whichever it was, we were enjoying the moment.

We were about two or three pitchers in, when one of my co-workers just jumped up from his seat. Everybody was startled and we asked if he's alright. He said, "Yeah man, I'm just tore up, I have to get on out of here. I need to pay this check and make it home, I'm just messed up, I need to go."

So I asked, "Hey you want us to get you an Uber or something? You straight? You need to be safe."

"No I'm alright, I'm just around the corner," he said, "but I'm going to be messed up in the morning."

So we agreed he'd better get home, and get sober since we all had to get in to work in the morning. Then he looked at us and said, "Work? What are you talking about work? Man, I'm calling in, once I get home." We told him that he can't call in because he's drunk. He said, "Man I'm not calling in because I'm drunk, I'm calling in because of the hangover I'm going to have in the morning. But get this, I'm just going to tell them I'm just sick."

I looked at him and said, "Dude, you can't do that." He said, "What you mean, I can't?" Then he took out his phone, dialed the number – at the bar mind you.

He dialed the number, and my phone rang.

There's only one thing worse than calling out sick ahead of time from a bar, and that is calling out sick and your boss is sitting right there, at the same bar, right next to you, drinking.

Here's my point: All this workplace social fraternization, or fellowshipping, has gotten out of hand. We have people working all day, all week, then leaving work and going out, hanging out two or three times a week, drinking, complaining, sharing their life stories. All of that stuff gets folded in together.

So what happens is, the stuff you do, on what you think is your personal time, eventually ends up in the workplace. Something as simple as you having a stomach virus or some issue with your kids (your personal life) gets back to the workplace, and people start intimating, "Ah, he's probably lying," or "He's out there partying too hard, staying out too late, or making some other bad decision." That ends up impacting your job.

And not just that. Over time, the decisions you make in your personal life start impacting your ability to work, and your so-called friends and buddies start acting differently towards you, or around you. They may never say anything to you, but they're saying something about you with each evolving life/work event. You can't socialize, "kick it," get drunk and then go to work with the same people.

RULE 3.8: Mind Your Business

I was always told that it takes 12 hours to mind my own business, and 12 hours to stay out of everyone else's. As men, this is a practice that we all should quickly adopt. There are few things that are despised more than a man that tattles on another man.

I'm reminded of a "tattling" experience that I had with an acquaintance of mine.

On this particular day, I was working at a local hotel. In the midst of my work activity, I saw a guy that I knew, in passing, leave a room with a woman that was not his wife. This woman was "low tier;" she was gutter level, terrible looking, just bad. Thirty minutes later I received a phone call from my ol' lady asking me which hotel I was in, and what I was doing.

"I'm working, I'm on a job. You know the type of work I do, and you know why I'd be at a hotel in the middle of the day!" I said with indignation, "Why are you calling me asking me these questions in the first place? "

Well, it would appear that the guy that I saw was so concerned about me squealing on him, that he preemptively called his wife. Except, he told her that he saw me coming out of a hotel hugged up with another woman. His wife, which is a friend of my wife, could not help but call her with the news.

The whole campaign was started because one man was concerned that another man was going to expose his game.

Men, this is unacceptable. It is inappropriate to publicly draw another man's personal behavior into question. If his behavior impacts you, then approach him directly. Hypothetically, I would have been wrong for saying something if I had. But, this guy was doubly wrong, in that he lied. Moreover, he lied about something that he should not have spoken about even if it were in fact true. Though consequences may emanate from our failure to speak, when saying something makes circumstances worse than saying nothing, then we should say nothing. Mind your business.

RULE 3.9: Just Because You Say It, Doesn't Make It So

Personally, I feel like everybody has a right to do what they need to do, to feel how they need to feel. Just as long as what you need to do does not adversely impact my quality of life. Now, that being said, you can't go around being mad at everybody else because they don't understand your methods.

Here is an example of what I'm referring to. Not long ago, I had the opportunity to hang out with my crew at the NBA Finals. It was game seven, we had courtside seats, and we were just having a ball. So halftime comes, and we all head out to "celebrity watch", and recharge on refreshments. Of course, it's shoulder to shoulder in the concession area. I'm standing next to two women and they're obviously a couple. One is substantially more masculine than the other, but that's neither here nor there. What happened next is what sent me spiraling into a state of confusion. Again, we're shoulder to shoulder, snug and tight. I go to adjust myself, and my hand mistakenly grazes the bottom of the masculine woman. I knew it could have been perceived as inappropriate, even though it was accidental, so I attempted to apologize. But before the air had the opportunity to escape my lungs and pass over my tongue and teeth to form an apology, she fires off at me.

This woman had the audacity to look at me and say, "Fool, don't be grabbing my ass. I ain't gay."

I'm thinking – "What?" I was left speechless, no way to rebut, no way to return a comment. I couldn't even apologize. What do you say to that? Why was she so upset? I simply bumped into her and attempted to apologize. But she was so offended because in some twisted way, me bumping into her called her masculinity into question.

So I was confused, and still am, to some degree.

Look, in life, you can identify as whatever, or whomever you want. You can set goals and claim victories as you choose. But, in the final analysis, facts must bear out your claims if you expect to be genuinely received. So, if you're walking around claiming to be an entrepreneur, but you haven't so much as secured a business license, you're probably not one. Or perhaps you've gotten in the habit of beating your chest, telling everybody that you're a grown man, yet you're still living with mother, and driving your girlfriend's car around all the time. Just because you claim something doesn't make it so. Facts must support your claims.

RULE 3.10: Keep the Main Thing the Main Thing

I've learned that when friends are struggling with life issues, it's of little benefit to pile on with the painful "I told you so." What's better is to simply exercise a measure of grace and compassion in empathizing with their plight.

Of course, as I stated in the very beginning, the purpose of *Mannishlaws* is not to indict anyone's behavior, but to highlight, and speak on male behaviors in a way that may help others avoid potential pitfalls and life crises. Sadly, many of our greatest mistakes and setbacks stem from a failure to "keep the main thing, the main thing." This inability to place the right priority on people – and things, to a lesser degree – can have catastrophic effects on our daily lives over time, ultimately placing us in circumstances that seem insurmountable at best.

To better illustrate this point, I'll share the story of Kinni, a very charismatic gentleman that I've known for years. Kinni shares a relationship with Tanja that is the envy of most men. Tanja cares deeply for Kinni. So much so, that she routinely buys him the most fashionable of apparel. She even makes certain that he has money to spend. I've personally witnessed her put $500-600 in his pocket on multiple occasions. What's more, Tanja even allows Kinni to roam all about town in her Maserati.

Now, I've never known a time when I was jealous of another man, but in this case, one has to wonder what would possess a woman to make that kind of financial and emotional investment in a man, especially when she knows he's married?

Yes, very married.

Again, I'm not hating, that's not what I do. But a reasonable man has to ask himself, "How can I get some of that?"

So, Kinni confides in me, sharing that things are not good with Tanja anymore. The relationship was as sweet as peaches and cream, and suddenly it went sour.

He tells me that he was at Tanja's house, they were having a good time, and she says, "Hey, I think it's about time you start spending the night, three or four nights a week." And he says, "How in the world can I do that when I have a family?"

"Do what you have to do," she says, "but you need to work it out."

He panicked, words were exchanged, and he left abruptly. Eventually he calmed down and went home, only to hear his doorbell ring about two o'clock in the morning. He opened his door to see a 3-foot-high pile of clothes on fire on his doorstep. She sat there in the driveway, in the Maserati, telling him to never come back. Now he's concerned, afraid and embarrassed, asking himself how he ever got in this predicament.

Well, believe it or not, this happens to many men, frequently. Perhaps not to the extent of having an extramarital affair go awry, but in the realm of experiencing substantial life setbacks because we misplace valuable resources, effort and attention.

Why?

Because we perceive the reward to be greater in some way. And while the reward may indeed be greater, we tend to find that the penalties are greater as well. To avoid pitfalls such as what was experienced by Kinni, you must stay focused on your prime target, and always remember why it's your target in the first place. You must keep the main thing the main thing.

RULE 3.11: You Play to Win

I was in the barbershop not long ago and remember an interesting conversation that was unfolding. We were talking about containing cost in our daily lives, and finding ways to get the greatest value when purchasing automobiles, clothes and home necessities. The genesis of the conversation was when one of the guys said that his car needed work and he was going to put it in the shop. Of course we asked where he was getting it serviced. He said the dealership. Upon hearing this, the shop erupted with everyone offering suggestions on reputable places to go to save money.

With the unexpected influx of recommendations on car service options, the guy responded by saying, "I'm not worried about saving money, I'll pay full price. I'll take it to the dealer so I don't have to worry about anything. I'm not big on trying to get discounts, or sale prices. My money ain't short. I'm staying true to the game."

As bizarre as his response was, it got me to thinking. What game is he staying true to? Is there a game that you win by paying more than you have to pay for something, just because you can?

So I thought further. And, I even said to the gentleman, "Is there a game out there that you win, by losing? And if so, is losing the new winning that makes you true to the game?"

He looked at me with a puzzled expression and asked me to explain myself, as did others in the shop. I went on to say that every game that I had observed in life shared a singular goal – to be won, not simply played, or stayed true to.

Now, as benign as his comments seemed, what he actually said was symptomatic of something much more malignant. A flawed mindset. An undisciplined thought process that says, "I can be irresponsible because I have the means to be."

Consider a game, in any competitive sport. One team is winning over the other with a substantial margin. Knowing that the other team has little chance of coming back to win, the team in the lead starts committing a range of penalties. Needless, unnecessary penalties. Now, some would say, "They still won, so the penalties are of no consequence." Well, perhaps, but suppose each penalty has a fine attached to it? That now affects the complexion of the win, doesn't it? Because, even though the team still won, the penalties made the win more costly.

Likewise, in life we can be in situations where success may be a constant, but the cost of success may be variable. So, why should we pay more, choose less, or simply be undisciplined, when we don't have to be?

In everyday life terms, this means it's not good enough to just attend school; you must graduate. Nor should you be content to just be in a relationship with somebody; the relationship should be a thriving and rewarding experience.

The bottom line is this: You don't play a game to participate, or be true to it, you play the game to win!

RULE 3.12: Don't Condition, Then Complain

If you're honest and open with yourself, and open your mind, you'll see the value and power in these rules. Not because they're new and unique, but to the contrary. Each of these rules represents basic life circumstances that we have all been involved in, or have observed someone close to us experience. There are so many things that we do on a daily basis that we waste the learning opportunity. We tend to condition ourselves, and people around us to respond to a particular stimulus in a particular way, then we complain at the outcome of the conditioning.

Here is one of the most basic, but common, of examples of conditioning and complaining.

There's a common phenomenon that takes place in many bars and social clubs. It involves men purchasing pitchers of beverages, then breaking their necks pouring it into the glasses of every half-way decent-looking woman that comes in proximity of them. They fill their glasses up the rest of the night as if that's going to guarantee some positive outcome. No guys, it's crazy, plain crazy – all you're doing is setting poor expectations for the future. Conditioning these same women to return for more free drinks.

Case in point: Last week, I stopped in at one of my regular spots to have a cocktail and grab a good seat. It was football night and I knew the seating would get scarce quickly. Not long after sitting down, a marginally attractive lady walks in the room. She bellies up to the bar and orders a shot of water – straight. That's right, a shot of water. She lets it sit there. She looks at me, I look at her, and it's just us, and a shot of water. About 10 minutes later, a couple brothers come walking in, they're big ballers (guys that like to openly spend money to appear well off), ordering a couple pitchers of margaritas a piece. Next thing you know, it's her and them in an engaging conversation. She's drinking out of both of their pitchers, having a great night, loud and rowdy, just having a real good time. So the evening progresses and the liquor continues to flow. Then, without warning, the lady says, "Oh, it's late, I've got to go." One of the "big ballers" replied, "Well, can I get your number? No? At least a hug, considering you've drank on me all night." The lady retorted, "All I owe you is a 'thank you,' and I've already given you that." Now some would say the baller was disappointed, others would say he was pissed. I'd say he was properly paid for his presumptuousness.

That was last week. Fast forward to yesterday. I walk into the same bar, the only dude in the room. This time there are eight women sitting around the bar with shots of water. Nobody's drinking, everybody's on their phone. But as soon as I came up, it was like time stopped – I looked at them, and they looked at me, as I sat down. Nobody's saying a word. Then the waiter comes to take my order, so, I order a pitcher of top-shelf margarita. Then all the sudden, everybody's talking, asking my name, telling me how attractive I am, don't I remember them from the old church? Or, where did I go to school? Was I in the military?

Stop it! This is crazy!

I share this example because it simply illustrates how, as men, we are eager to condition women to expect a reward without the requirements of any type of performance. Now, I'm not saying that there should be some sort of "quid pro quo" for a glass of wine. But what I am saying is that men must stop collectively conditioning women to expect a reward, without contributing, then being upset when no contribution is made.

Keep in mind, the example used in this rule is a template that is easily overlaid in other aspects of life. Let's take this example out of the social club and consider the following:

• Are we in relationships where we condition our partners to expect a reward, even when they are not healthy, equitable contributors? Then do we complain that they aren't meeting our needs?

• Do we reward our children with excess, when they simply do what they're supposed to do, then complain that they aren't achievers?

• Do we work on jobs in which we pour all of our energy and effort into it, only to hear that business is tough, so no raises will be given? And still we work there, with no plan for leaving for greener pastures. We just complain about feeling devalued.

In the bar scene, the rule is pretty clear. You can't be buying these women drinks in perpetuity, without some clear expectation or requirement being placed on them. Otherwise, every woman in the world is going to be walking up in these bars ordering water straight up, expecting to drink out of the next brother's pitcher. Leaving us with no recourse outside of complaining.

Likewise, in other areas of life, if we continue to perform with no requirement of reward from others, we'll always find ourselves, disappointed and unfulfilled, but full of complaints. We can't have that. If the world is drinking out of your pitcher, you best believe that the world should put something on it.

RULE 3.13: Nine Words of Death

"If you would just let me be the man."

Those are nine words that no man should find himself in the situation to ever say. I get it though – life brings circumstances that causes us to say, and do, things that sometimes we look back on and regret. But these nine words ... there is no circumstance so dire, no issue so extreme, no pressure so pressing, that should cause us to say them.

A close friend of mine recently uttered these words, and I've not been able to look at him the same.

After having a stressful day at work, he went home, and as soon as he walked through the door, his old lady pounced on him, with some level of conflict. Already stressed, he was unprepared to respond appropriately, and as a result, he uttered those nine words of death: "If you would just let me be the man."

If you would just let me be the man?

This statement is bone-crushing, earth-shattering. Nine words of devastation that no true man should ever find himself saying.

Even in the midst of the conflict, he didn't realize what he had done.

He failed to recognize that when you say "If you would just let me be the man" you have conceded the right that God has given you from birth. No one can allow you to take advantage of a God-given right, unless you forfeit it, or fail to live up to it. And even when you utter those words, there's only one thing worse that can happen: you have to listen to her say, "Okay, you're the man." Wow! And that's exactly what she said to him.

"How do you feel about this experience?" I asked him. Blindly, he said he thought they were on the road to recovery.

I find myself saddened because this guy is lost, and doesn't even understand the significance, or the extreme of what he's done. His manhood is dead and buried. Don't get me wrong, I still respect him, but not with the same energy that I had in the past. I respect him with the same type of minimalistic respect I show to any human being, that stranger I open the door for when I walk into a building.

His life is not the same. His woman can't look at him the same way, because the Queen has just given permission to the King to sit on the throne. Now, if the Queen orders the King, is there really a king? So I mourn the death of his manhood.

The thing that really gets me is that this guy is just one of many men out there trying to negotiate their God-given position and range of responsibilities. They're saying to some woman, "If you'll only let me ... if you'll allow me ... if you would just settle down, baby please." What is it that possesses a man to forfeit the very essence of who he is? We all need to understand that there is no coming back from that point. Once you forfeit your right and position as a man, how do you regain it? You're telling this woman that you're no longer the man, but you're the man she approves you to be. And if you have kids, you can no longer be the father you were aspiring to be. You can no longer be the committed life partner, the husband, that you hoped to be. You can no longer please and satisfy your woman to the extent that you once had, because those nine words compromised and sacrificed everything that you had been – and hoped to be – before you uttered them.

I mourn because he's just one example of what's going on, on a daily basis. This has to stop; we've got to revolt. As men, we must resist that demonic voice within that presents the Nine Words of Death as a possible response in any conversation. Men, you must commit to never say those words. Whether it's a fear of loneliness, fear of alienation, no sex, not wanting to listen to her mouth – it doesn't matter. Say nothing, or say anything else but those nine words. Once you do, you can't get your manhood back. Once you allow a woman to approve your manhood, you're dead.

RULE 3.14: "Facetiming" is Reckless

When it comes to technology I consider myself one of the most technologically savvy people you're ever going to meet. If it involves the latest smart device or software upgrades, I'm probably walking around with it in my pocket. Even still, I recognize that there comes a point when we just have to pump our brakes and say, "Enough is enough."

I consider this whole Facetime video chat activity to be an example of enough being enough. We're now living in an era where people are walking down the street and being mowed down by cars, simply because they're so involved in their Facetime conversation that they're not even aware of their surroundings. This is a problem of great concern.

Moreover, when you introduce Facetime and other video chat applications into your personal relationships, you set the expectation that you are as available visually as you are over voice.

In fact, just the other night I attended a "Members Only" social gathering. For the purposes of this reading, "Members Only" is code for a group of my buddies having a private party with female entertainers. Nevertheless, during the activities, one of the guys gets an incoming Facetime call from his spouse. I'm thinking, why is he getting a Facetime during our social gathering? He answers the call, and two minutes into the call I hear her say, "Pan the room."

Pan the room?

What exactly does "pan the room" mean? Well, he turns the camera around and shows her the entire room.

First, please understand that when you get an incoming video call from your girl, your significant other or your spouse, it's not because they miss you so much that they need to make a visual connection. No, they're Facetiming you because they want to see where you are, and who you're with.

Now, back to the guy at the event. When he panned the room, his spouse saw a good example of men behaving badly in the mist of entertainers with naked body parts jiggling and wiggling – it was a hell of a "Member's Only" meeting, if I do say so myself. Fast forward, and over the last three weeks he's been staying with me because his wife is still pretty hot.

Here's the lesson that must be recognized: Men, if you're Facetiming all the time, you're either needy or stupid. By frequently Facetiming your girl, you'll quickly condition her to think that it's okay to video chat with you whenever she gets the urge. That would be the stupid part. Because, all you're doing is setting yourself up for problems down the road, as inevitably there will be occasions when you won't want to be seen. Only heard.

RULE 3.15: No Joint Bank Accounts

Being in love, or even being in like in some cases, can be a wonderful thing. It's something everybody should have the opportunity to experience. But you can't let love or even infatuation be the reason you make poor or irrational decisions in your relationship. I often advise men against making quick, emotion-based decisions, but oftentimes the result is the same. They don't want to listen to wisdom.

Take my friend Jack. He mentioned that he's seeing a woman (Jill), that he considered to be special. He said their feelings for each other were so strong, that they were going to do the right thing. I congratulated him and asked about the wedding.

"We're not getting married," he said. "We're going to get a joint bank account. We're going to pool our money, so we can realize the American Dream."

My response: "Man, are you crazy? A joint bank account? You're losing your mind – that's the kiss of death."

He didn't want to listen, so Jack and Jill ran up the hill and got a joint bank account. Now Jack's staying at an extended stay motel, pouting, because he doesn't want to explain the $200 that left the joint bank account. Or the $180 purchase at Men's Warehouse. Or the $170 purchase at the Hyatt Hotel. It turns out that he can't go home until he's willing to explain where that money went.

Consider this: You can do a lot of things together in a relationship, but resist having a joint bank account. Not only will this shared account itemize your spending history, but it can also reduce your freedom to spend without scrutiny or objection. The questions you must ask include:

- "Why do I need my spending scrutinized or questioned?"

- "Is this a requirement for this relationship to prosper?"

- "What other options do we have, other than a joint account?"

Ultimately, the goal should be in doing and accomplishing things together. But, is any of that predicated on a joint account?

PART FOUR

RELATING TO WOMEN

A wise man by the name of Desiderius Erasmus, once wrote, "Women ... Can't live with them. Can't live without them." Truer words have never been spoken. But why is this the case? Is it because the true understanding of women rests beyond the conceptual boundaries of men? Hmm ... could be ... but probably not. I'd like to offer another explanation that may speak more clearly to the inherent complexities of the male-female relationship. I'll do this, in part, by sharing a story that we've all heard before. But for the sake of brevity, I'll skip over some of the details.

The story begins with two deities having a conversation about creating a lesser being in their image. Ultimately they did create this being, it was a human. They called this human "man." This man was unique among all creatures created, and he was the very first of his kind. Because he was made in their image, they gave him the awesome responsibility of managing all things in the kingdom. He had dominion over every single thing. I'm thinking that made him the very first king. This was a great responsibility for him, and as you can imagine, a lot of work was involved. But even still, there were times that he was idle and lonely. The deities recognized this and said, "Hey, let's create a companion for this man."

And they did. They caused a great sleep to come upon him, and at this point they took a rib from his side. Now, I don't know about you, but I'm thinking this had to be a painful process. We're talking about a time where there was no propofol, no hydrocodone, no morphine or any other pain-relieving agents to be found. But nevertheless, they were successful in creating a helpmate for him. They called this slightly lesser human "woman" because she was taken from the man.

So that's how the story went in a nutshell, but this is where the learning actually begins. To understand the dynamics in the male-female relationship, you must consider what I like to call "The Rib Complex."

In the body, the ribs are responsible for protecting all of the most vital organs. The organs that are essential to sustaining life. When a man faces conflict, or battle, one of the key areas that he always seeks to protect is the rib cage, or the torso. He is protecting that which is protecting what is essential to life. So in this example, the man should find himself protecting the woman, who would be the rib, because she in turn would be protecting those vital and important things in his life.

Now, on the flip side, the woman, or the rib, is always going to find herself wanting to be an important part of something bigger. She's going to want to feel valuable, and protected. She's also going to want to be a contributor to the safety and well-being of the man.

Now if we consider those two perspectives, they seem to go well together and are easily reconciled. So why do we still have so many issues and complexities in our relationships? In a word, it boils down to compatibility.

Compatibility, or the aspect of "fitting together," makes all the difference in the success and health of a relationship. When we consider the rib, if it's a touch too small, a lot goes lacking. There's not enough coverage to protect all that's important. Conversely a rib too large may provide all of the protective coverage that you need, but not without agonizing pain in the side.

So, to wrap a bow around this, to achieve the healthiest, most fulfilling relationships, compatibility must be considered ahead of many other desires and characteristics.

In Section 4, we'll spend our time talking about issues and observations of the male-female interaction. We'll see examples of life circumstances that may be valuable learnings that we can leverage to better cope with our female partners, inside and outside of relationships.

RULE 4.1: Date for Substance, not Circumstance

I think we all may be familiar with the phrase, "opposites attract." And while it's true, it's only a good thing if you are a magnet. When you are talking about two or more individuals getting together to form a relationship, like charges are more desirable. People with similar interests are going to have more in common, which means they will have an opportunity to enjoy more activities together.

Take this as an extreme example: Two crackheads are dating, and really enjoying life as they know it. They're having a great time, as all they do is smoke crack, drink and have sex. Right up until one day the lady decides she doesn't want to smoke crack anymore. She thinks the habit is causing her to use poor judgement in making life choices.

Well okay, thinks her guy. We can still drink and have great sex. Except for the fact that she also didn't want to drink anymore. She was only drinking because it went along with the feeling that she had from smoking crack. Now her boyfriend, who is still committed to the crackhead way, is thinking, "Well, I can still smoke crack, and I can drink, and the two of us can still have great sex." Well, that's not a thing anymore either. Truth is, she was only having sex with the guy because she was drunk and high. Now that she is sober, she is seeing him, and so many other things, in a different light.

I share this example because it is not an uncommon phenomenon for people to find themselves in relationships that are born out of circumstance. Whether fortunate or not, life events have been known to set the stage for people to meet and partner in relationships on a range of levels and length. Of course, I'm not saying that these relationships can't work. However, I am suggesting that relationships based more on commonalities, than the circumstances that brought you together, are likely to be healthier, more fulfilling, and more enriching. For this reason, it is important to date for qualitative, as well as quantitative substance. Qualitative from the standpoint that you need to look for non-superficial characteristics that will bring value to your relationship now, as well as in the future. Quantitative, from the standpoint that you need as many things in common as possible, as those will be the things that you will do together and enjoy doing alone as well. If you have 10 things in common and you decide that you don't want to do two of them anymore, that's okay because now you still have eight things that you can enjoy doing together. So, remember, date for substance rather than circumstance.

RULE 4.2: Compatibility Breeds Longevity

Whether we admit it or not, we all seek "happily ever after" to some degree. For some of us, it is simply "happily ever after" – now. When it comes to relationships, we look for many things in the people that we hope to share time, and even life with. Good looks, good jobs, material achievements, kids, no kids. All of these characteristics are factors that have come to be important to us based on our life and relationship experiences.

Unfortunately, we often believe that these characteristics are what overwhelmingly determines the likelihood of a relationship being successful. The problem is when we put so much weight on these, and other similar external characteristics, we tend to minimize the importance of those internal factors that actually define who people are. If you don't invest time in discovering the character of a person, how can you determine whether you are compatible?

When we decide to investigate core compatibility, we must basically ask ourselves whether this person is a good fit for me, and me for them.

Compatibility sets the stage for longevity, because as we mentioned in RULE 4.2, the things that you have in common will be the things that you do going forward.

This thought reminds me of the story of Michealas. I met him one day for lunch, and he was decidedly ecstatic. Understand that he is usually a mild-mannered, quiet guy, to say the least. Typically, he would rather respond to your comments more than initiate conversation. But on this day, Michealas was bubbling with words to say.

So I had to ask, "Michealas, what's gotten into you? You have so much energy, what's going on?" He then told me that he had met a lady, and he was sure that she would prove to be his happily ever after. Me being puzzled, I probed for more. I asked, "What makes her so special, and how can you be sure this is a happily ever after?"

He tells me that this lady is a professional woman, an executive with a major international company. She is also an entrepreneur with a budding business of her own. She has several properties, and a few really nice cars. She also loves to travel out of the country and experience new things.

Well at this point, I'm biting my tongue with all my might. I'm trying not to say or ask anything that may be in opposition to his vision of his "happily ever after." But, truth be told, I could not contain myself any longer.

I asked Michealas, "Why do you think this is a happily-ever-after situation?" He said, "I just told you. This is someone I've been waiting for. She is the catch of a lifetime." He then asked me why I seemed so doubtful. I responded by asking him if he really wanted a happily ever after. He said he did. So, I told him to move on, as this probably wasn't the woman for him. Now he looked puzzled.

I went on to tell him, "Michealas, you don't travel. You don't like to experience new things, as you have a conspiracy theory about everything. You can't go out of the country because you don't have a passport. Even if you did go out of the country, when you attempted to return, you would be detained because of your outstanding warrants and delinquent child support. Furthermore, you have not demonstrated an ability to keep a job for more than a few months at a time. In your 43 years of life, you have not accumulated anything more than a $3,000 minivan. You're still living with your parents when you're not living with a roommate. So, when you consider the things that I have mentioned, what about you would make her want you as her happily ever after? You lack compatibility on virtually every level beyond the ability to discuss current events."

He looked at me and said, "There's more to life than that stuff." Yet she was his "happily ever after" because of all her "stuff."

Clearly, he didn't get it. Sure, there was obviously some type of attraction between the two. Who's to say how far the attraction would go? But, one thing is for sure: Once they advance beyond the initial attraction, they'll see what they have in common, what very little there actually is. For this reason, it is essential to seek compatibility if you want longevity.

RULE 4.3: Financial Compatibility is Important

I'm all for a man outwardly demonstrating love for his woman. I believe that you should do your very best to treat her like a queen. This means you're always handling her with a spirit of love and respect.

At the same time, you have to consider financial compatibility when it comes to dating. You must be equally yoked. I was recently in a Men's Ministry meeting at church, when a member expressed concerns about feeling less than his woman. While he was deeply in love with her, the fact that her income is ten times greater than his was the source of great stress for him.

And while others in the ministry offered prayer and words of support, I felt compelled to tell him the truth: "You're on borrowed time. There is no way you're going to be able to support this woman financially, or meet her expectations over time, on things that require money. Not to say that you aren't compatible in other areas, but she makes ten times as much as you, which means her expectations are probably ten times greater than you're able to reach. Now, perhaps she does love you, and she's able to look past that. Still, how are you going to be able to keep her stimulated and involved if your resources are ten times less than her expectations? Are we to think that she'll down-regulate her desires and expectations from now on? She might – but probably won't. Or, would you be content with her footing the bill for the majority of things that the two of you do in the relationship?"

Now, I'd liked to think that this was going to be a "happily ever after" for him. But my gut reaction was that he was on borrowed time.

The bottom line is that you've got to have a level of financial compatibility that is balanced and based in realism. You can date somebody that's a few tiers above where you are financially, when the numbers are relatively small. People make those types of relationships work every day. But when there is a substantial gap, or chasm, in earnings, odds are you're going to have a series of finance-based issues that revolve around one person's expectations exceeding the other person's ability or willingness to provide.

RULE 4.4: Create a Culture of Praise and Recognition

Insecurity is that substance that can make the strongest of relationships crumble under its own weight. Earlier I spoke about the rib complex of a woman. The need to feel valued, important and a part of something greater. Creating a culture of praise and recognition is one of the best ways to ensure that a woman understands the importance of her role in a relationship. Expressing words of praise and recognition for the smallest things provide a great opportunity to highlight the importance of what she contributes, while setting an expectation of more good things to come.

RULE 4.5: Give Credit When It's Not Due

Being the man in a relationship, or simply the leader in the family, does not mean that you have to have all the right answers, all the time. Nor does it mean accepting all the credit all the time. Ultimately, in your relationship, when things go well (or badly), all eyes are going to land on you.

For this reason, be the first to accept responsibility when things don't go as well as they could, but when they do, use this time as an opportunity to lift her up for her contributions to the success. This isn't necessary in every case, but in some cases even where it's not truly deserved, you'll find yourself building higher levels of goodwill and appreciation.

The process of self-development and relationship growth requires extensive work. And while you can improve you in your self-development, you can't build up your relationship without finding opportunities to build your partner up. This recognition will pay dividends in the future.

RULE 4.6: Beating Your Chest Will Leave You Sore

It's something to be said for being correct. For doing the right thing. For being in charge and bearing responsibility. These things are truly important. And, if you find yourself doing these things with any level of consistency, everyone will recognize it. No, it won't always be acknowledged openly, but it will certainly be noticed by those around you, especially those that benefit.

So, get in the habit of simply doing what's required, or what needs to be done, and letting that stand for itself rather than beating your chest to bring attention to your efforts.

Constantly beating your chest to gain recognition for doing what you're supposed to be doing will ultimately leave you fatigued. It will also gain you attention that is counter to what you're looking for.

RULE 4.7: Exercise Grace, Forgiveness and Flexibility

If you live long enough you'll find that you're going to have disagreements. Disagreements don't necessarily mean that one person is a good person and the other is bad; they simply mean that people don't see things the same way. Understanding this, it's a good practice to exercise grace and flexibility wherever and whenever you can, especially when attempting to resolve conflict.

This means that after the disagreement, you need to make it easy for someone to come over to your side of the discussion.

I remember an occasion when two buddies of mine, Al and Jessuca, were having a heated exchange. Al was being overly critical of the color palettes that his spouse Jessuca chose for the entertainment room in their new home. Jessuca felt insulted by Al's criticism as she saw nothing wrong with an orange-and-blue color theme. However, in time she came to realize that the colors she selected were the colors of Al's favorite college football team's arch rival. Finally understanding the source of Al's contempt, she softened her position and offered an apology.

Al, who was so relieved that the feuding was about to be settled, thanked Jessuca for exercising common decency and good sense.

So, just to be clear, he was mad about her initial choice; she relents and opens to compromise; he then insults her even more.

Now what happens?

Well, it's two years later, and the entertainment room is still white with no new paint job. As men, even in the midst of arguments and disagreements, we must remember the goal. We must stay focused on the point of the discussion, or the aim of the movement, and do our best to make it easy for others to feel like they made the right choice in coming around to our way of thought. This often involves demonstrating grace, forgiveness or flexibility. Each time we take advantage of an opportunity to emphasize how right we are, by belittling others, we often end up further away from our goal.

RULE 4.8: Care About More Than You

I was talking to a young man just the other day, and he was expressing a level of frustration with the way his life was turning out. I probed him, asking specific questions, hoping to get to the root of his malcontent. But, he seemed disinterested, or unable to answer the most basic questions surrounding his life challenges. There was, however, a common theme. I'd asked a question, and the young man would respond with:

- "I don't know,"

- "I really don't care," or

- "I'm just out here trying to get mine."

My response, in the most polite way I knew how, was to ask, "How's that working out for you? The part about not knowing, and not caring?" He said, "It's working out fine." "Well, if that's the case, why all of the frustration?"

So as the conversation evolved, I came to understand the source of his issues, a problem that is all too common among young men. Poor spatial recognition, an inability to identify "cause-effect," "if-then" relationships associated with his behaviors and life decisions. So no, things weren't actually going the way that he desired, and odds are, they probably weren't going to go his way for a while.

I shared with the young man that it's absolutely okay to be angry, frustrated and disappointed with life results. All of those feelings are natural in the process of growth. But, growth cannot be achieved without recognizing, and addressing, the "cause-effect" components.

The fact is, you have to come to a point in your life where you recognize that there are very important things in the world, outside of you, that affect you. Since none of us have overwhelming control of all of the circumstances that allow us to succeed, or fail, we must consider that there are some things outside of our control. Things that directly impact our lives. Not only is it advantageous to know what these things are, it is essential to care about these things, or people, to some degree. So, the thought process of "I don't care" just doesn't work. It can't work. You must care about things and people outside of you.

RULE 4.9: Do, or Don't. But Stop With All the Trying.

I'm a huge sci-fi fan. *Star Wars*, *Star Trek*, *Battlestar Galactica*, and a range of other lesser-known movies and series – I can even go back to *Buck Rogers in the 25th Century*. Unfortunately, I feel like I'm dating myself. But there is a quote that is specific to one of the *Star Wars* movies that I try to live by on a daily basis. There was a scene in *The Empire Strikes*

Back where Luke Skywalker is being instructed on leveraging the force to do incredible things. He's told by the Jedi Master to use the force to lift his spacecraft out of the murky swamp. Luke Skywalker concentrates, stands, raises his hands, and tries and tries. He can feel the force within him bubbling up, and he sees the spacecraft starting to come out of the water. Then all of a sudden, the spacecraft collapses even deeper than it originally was. Luke says it's too big. The Jedi Master looks down and with disappointment said nothing is too big, or something along those lines. Luke's response: Look I tried, I did my best. And what comes out of his Jedi Master's mouth is something I've used in coaching and mentoring time, and time again. Yoda, the ancient Jedi Master replied, "Do, or don't do. There is no try."

I consider this to be one of the most powerful statements I've ever heard in the realm of coaching and development. How many people have you dealt with in your life that are always trying to do something? Trying to get involved in the new business opportunity, trying to get their degree, trying to build something – trying, trying, trying – yet they ultimately have very little to show for it in the range of victories or successes. If you don't know anyone that fits this description, then you are probably that person.

We all know that failure is, yes, a real thing. But it does not have to be an option. You can choose to do something, or decide not to. When you get caught up in the loop of trying, you're actually going backwards. Backwards because you're putting in a lot of repetitive energy that is netting you nothing. So, if you find yourself constantly trying, but not having anything to show for it, you need to ask yourself some very serious and specific questions. You also need to develop a mentor/mentee relationship with someone that can assist you in becoming more aware of any resources that are available to aid in your growth, as well as help you discover your developmental gaps. Furthermore, you must uncover what things are serving as the impediments to you achieving the goals that you're constantly finding yourself trying to accomplish.

In your relationships, the same thing applies. You can't always be:

- Trying to be a better man

- Trying to find a better job

- Trying to be more attentive

- Trying to be the head of the house

At some point, you have to demonstrate these behaviors if you want your value as a man to be recognized and appreciated.

RULE 4.10: Don't Justify a Failure

In life, you'll find that you'll tend to gain notoriety and a reputation by the things that people observe you doing. The work that you do, the car that you drive, the things that you get involved with in the community. A lot of things that are audible or visual will go a long way in sending a message about you and your brand. But understand this: your failure to do things will send a message that is just as clear, or even clearer, than the messages sent by the things that you are involved with.

When people see value in you and respect your brand, they grow to have certain expectations of you. Moreover, when you're important in the lives of people, and they are dependent on you for sustenance, they begin to put confidence in what they believe you will do – or won't do. And in some cases, your responses can be of critical impact.

So, when you commit to someone that you will do something, and you fail to do it, what impact does that have, and what message does that send to them about your integrity and ability to keep your word?

I remember having a conversation with a gentleman that was in my employ. He was upset about a lady friend with whom he just finished having an argument. It seems that the lady mentioned that she needed to get her hair done, so she wasn't going to be able to go out with him the upcoming weekend. This guy said, "Okay, you have to get your hair done. Well, Thursday I get paid and I'll give you something on it." What results from this is the young lady waits on him to meet her for the financial gift for her hair appointment. He doesn't show up, and he doesn't call. Eventually they do meet up on another day, and the young lady is furious. As the story was being told to me, my employee was growing irritated. He felt as though she had no right to be upset with him.

I told him, "Friend, you don't get it."

He felt that she had to get her hair done anyway. Whether he helped, or not. So, he figured, she shouldn't be mad at him for not giving her money. After some more back and forth, I was finally successful in making him understand that the lady was upset at the fact that he said he was going to do something, and he failed to keep his word. Not only did he fail to follow through, but he didn't even have the courage and integrity to call and notify her.

The hit that your integrity takes from this type of miscue, can be difficult to overcome. A substantial part of learning from failures, is learning how to properly deal with the failure itself. In some cases, the failure may not be as extreme as the potential repercussions from not effectively addressing it. So, if you find yourself in a situation where things are not going to work out the way you had planned, what do you do? And, who do you tell?

Just remember that it is important that you demonstrate the responsibility and the integrity to address your change of mind head on. People have to know where you stand, and where they stand with you. The worst thing that you can do is to justify a failure.

RULE 4.11: Never Seek Permission

One of the most bizarre observations that I have made among guys recently, is the phenomenon of permission seeking. Defining, and explaining this phenomenon is difficult, but I'll try my best.

In fact, I'll use an example that happened to me a few years ago. It went like this: I picked up a phone call from a buddy of mine, he was calling to coordinate a happy hour outing. We agreed on a spot and a time, but he then said that he was just about to walk into the house. He requested that I give him a call back in about 5 minutes. While this struck me as a bit odd, I didn't think that much of it. I hung up, and 5 minutes later called him back. He answered the phone and started talking to me as if we hadn't talked in years.

So I asked, "Man are you coming out or what?"

He said, "Yeah, that sounds good, hang on a minute." He then said to his wife, "Hey honey, Solomon is calling me and asking me out for happy hour. Is that okay with you?"

She responded, "Where are y'all going?"

"Hadn't decided yet," he said sheepishly

She responded indifferently with, "Okay, but let me know where you go, so I'll know if I want you to bring me something back."

Wrong! Wrong! Wrong! On so many levels!

First off, I have no problem with a guy communicating with his spouse, or partner on what he is about to do. Or even asking if anything is going on in the household that might conflict with him going out. But asking permission to go out, or to do something, is waiving your God-given right as an adult. You further exacerbate this by waiting on her to decide whether it's okay, based on where you say you're going.

And then lastly, allowing her to require that you call her once you get there adds insult to misery. Look, you cannot be a man and allow yourself to report, check in, and communicate as if you are a child.

"Hey honey, do we have anything planned this evening? No, great, Solomon and I are going out to have a few drinks. I should be back a little bit later." That's what good communication looks like.

It should be noted that when the lady "requires" to know where her man is going or doing when he's essentially not at home or at work, boils down to three things: a lack of trust, a control issue on the lady's part, or general insecurity on her part. Of course, for the man to allow it means he's acquiescing. All these things point to issues that should be addressed with each side of the relationship. If it's a trust issue, take care of it. If an insecurity or control issue, she must address it.

Bottom line: If this phenomenon is part of your life, handle it appropriately by taking charge and nixing the problem.

RULE 4.12: Make Your Standard the Deal-breaker

Earlier, I talked about having standards and expectations in place for yourself, rather than imposed by others. This is something that's huge as part of being a man. Because you are known by your brand, living by your brand should not be dictated by others, due to your failure to frame it properly. That being said, when you have standards and expectations, they can't just be your standards; they have to be accepted and adhered to by those you are involved with and responsible for.

If you believe there is a particular way that is acceptable to dress, speak or simply carry yourself in public, you can't allow your lady to violate that standard when she leaves the house. Your standard must be the standard for both of you. There has to be a threshold for what is acceptable and what is not. If her standards are lower than yours, she has to raise them. If yours are lower than hers, you have to elevate yours. Your standards must be adhered to. If this is something that can't be done, for whatever reason, you must recognize that you have an issue of compatibility.

RULE 4.13: Don't be Afraid to do Without

An important question: What stops you from doing certain things?

Do you know what stops you from getting that extra brownie, saying hello to the pretty receptionist on the fifth floor, or driving 85 in a 55, and so on? More times than not it is that concern that we have with losing – you know, having something stripped from us. In rare cases it is a concern that something will be added to us, but ultimately whatever's added is punitive in nature. So, in our mind, we skip the extra brownie because we're afraid it may add to our waist size, which means we won't fit into our favorite pants. We won't say hello to Melissa, the superhot receptionist upstairs, because she knows our girlfriend's sister. And we certainly don't want that getting back. And speeding, well, that's just a whole other thing. Thirty miles over the speed limit equates to reckless driving, mandatory jail time and inflated insurance rates, which all boils down to money coming out of our pockets. So, with these three examples I understand why most people are afraid to do certain things.

But, even with those examples in mind, we can't let fear of doing without manage our world. When it comes to relationships, the fear of doing without oftentimes restricts us to our own peril. And women know that they are the one thing that most men do not want to "do without." Therefore, "doing without" becomes the number-one thing on the chopping block when women need leverage in our life. A common modus operandi is: So do that, or be prepared to do without this.

Regardless of the circumstances, if the threshold has been met, you'll have to develop the courage to be okay with doing without.

Now understand that on a case-by-case basis, doing without will certainly be more, or less challenging. You may have to do without the good-night phone call, support for a cause, or even do without a warm body in the bed next to you.

But ultimately, overcoming your fear of doing without, will make you better, stronger and more secure in who you are and what you stand for. It will also garner you a higher level of respect from that woman in your life.

RULE 4.14: Keep the Conflict About the Issue

I once ended a relationship over a camcorder purchased in New York.

I was doing the whole tourist thing when I walked up on one of those street vendors peddling electronics. He offered me a great deal on a Sony camcorder. He demonstrated one, and I was pretty impressed with it, plus the price was right. So, I bought it. When I got back to my hotel room and opened the box, it was full of wet newspaper in a big Ziploc bag. Needless to say I was pissed! The lady that I was traveling with at that time asked, "Why did you buy that anyway?" I said the guy said that it was brand new and he offered me a good deal, $150.

Nuclear Moment Begins – she looked me in my eyes and asked, "So you thought you could get a $900 camcorder for $150? You're just stupid enough to believe that."

From that statement, the interaction spun out of control until we simply agreed to stop talking for a while. Ultimately, I was hardly upset about being taken advantage of with the purchase. I was more aggravated at the fact that she called me stupid, as well as some of the other things that were said in our verbal altercation. We found ourselves flinging insults back and forth, insults that had very little – actually nothing – to do with the issue at hand.

How common is this? People have a disagreement and an argument develops that involves a whole lot of rhetoric that has very little to do with the facts of the disagreement. Things get said, feelings get hurt, and people often apologize for things that they very often don't recover from.

That being said, remember, conflict is inevitable, so we have to be better managers of it. One of the best ways to do this is remembering to keep conflict about the issue and not about the person.

RULE 4.15: Expect Baggage, but Manage Drama

"I am drama free. I don't do drama." I can't tell you how many times I have heard ladies say this, or some variation. Usually speaking in the context of dating someone, these comments are generally used to set expectations for the hearer that "I'm really not interested in having any conflict, or being affected by the headaches of your past."

Imagine taking a trip across the country for a day, a week, a year – in fact, you can pick the time frame. The catch is that you may not take anything with you, regardless of how long the trip is. What's more, you can't bring anything back with you. And you can't share your travel plans. How difficult would that be? As impossible, or improbable, as it may seem to do such a thing, that's exactly what we are asking people to do when we tell them that we don't do drama. It is super important to understand that drama does not happen in a vacuum – drama is always the result of something else, usually related to situational or circumstantial conflict, that people may not agree on.

Consider this: You just got in from work, you walk in, kick off you shoes at the door and toss your briefcase on the sofa. None of which is a big deal. You have just come in and dropped your baggage, and all is okay. Well, not so much. What happens when someone is walking in the door at 11 p.m. and they stumble over your shoes? Or perhaps someone needs to sit on the sofa, but your briefcase is taking up space. You see, as basic as this example is, it shows that you have baggage in the simplest areas of life. Our baggage only becomes dramatic when someone else feels adversely impacted by having to deal with it. And "adversely" is certainly the key word, because I can't ever remember anyone complaining about any benefits of another's past.

The key is to understand that we all have accumulated emotional and material baggage based on our life experiences. What we must learn to do is effectively manage the dramatic interaction that we have with the baggage of another.

RULE 4.16: Set the Parameters of Your Relationship Early

I'm reminded of the story of Jack and Dionne. The two had a very secretive but passionate office romance.

In the very beginning of the flame, Dionne said to Jack, "I hope you understand where we are. We are both in committed relationships, so where we are is the most that we can ever be."

Jack nodded in agreement and said, "Let's just enjoy it while it lasts."

So time goes by and life happened. Dionne ended up deciding that her marriage was not viable anymore. So, she divorced. With the newness of her divorce, perspective on her relationship with Jack changed dramatically.

She told Jack one day, at the end of a passionate interlude, "I think I want us full-time."

Jack looked at her and said, "There's a zero-percent chance of that happening. You knew what this was when we started."

She answered, "I knew what it was when we started, but this right here isn't what that was."

At this point, Jack was forced into making a tough stand with Dionne by telling her that he is not interested, or able, to go any further with their relationship, than where they were. In no uncertain terms was he going to end his relationship with the person he was committed to.

I share this story because it happens quite often that people get involved and they allow the relationship to manage their lives. A lot of relationships grow and morph to whatever they become with no defined parameters or restrictions. Now, this is okay if both people are in agreement, but if one person has limits that are not set forth in the beginning of the relationship, then that person is going to be impacted once those limits are met. Also, the other person is going to feel slighted because they had no idea that these limits were in place.

By setting parameters early, both understand what the limits are even if someone's mind changes. They know what the constraints are that were agreed upon, and they know what the relationship boundaries are, even if they desire the boundaries to be changed. Parameters have to be set in the beginning.

RULE 4.17: Clear, Honest Communication is Essential

From time to time I experience emotional lows – depression, moodiness – just like any normal human being. I tend to cope by withdrawing into myself and finding a quiet place. I, for one, don't like to share my low moments as I believe that bad news can only be multiplied, not divided. So, I fight through it the best way I can.

But on one particular day, my lady came in and saw me sitting in a dark room, sipping on a cocktail and listening to a little music.

"What's going on?" she asked. "Are you depressed or something?"

I said, "No, I'm not depressed, I'm just trying to get my thought patterns back on track."

She said, "Well I need to know what's going on."

"Babe, everything's good."

"No, I'm sick of you being so emotionally unavailable. And if this relationship has any chance for the future, you're going to have to feel comfortable and free enough to tell me your deepest, darkest secrets and concerns."

I said, "Wow. I've got to tell you my deepest, darkest secrets and concerns? Right now?"

"Yeah!"

I took a deep breath, looked into her eyes, and told her, "Look, we're in a bad place. We've got some serious problems, and I don't even know if we're going to make it through."

She said, "Really? We're in that bad of a situation?"

I said, "Hell yeah, it's critical. First of all, we lost our starting quarterback, and our star running back. Our safety tore his ACL. And we've got a whole bunch of freshmen on the defensive line. Hell, I think our whole season is lost. We have no chance of playing in the college football playoffs the way things are going. I just don't know what to say."

She looked at me, turned around and just walked away. She didn't talk to me for three days.

Bottom line is this guys: Clear communication is the best thing for your relationship. You've got to be honest. Tell your women exactly what's on your mind and how you feel – your relationship will be much better off. There may be consequences, but ultimately you'll be so much better off. At least you'll have a lot more peace.

RULE 4.18: Manage your Expectations of Her

I'm a firm believer that women are the masters of over-promising and under-delivering. I say this because I've experienced this in many different areas and stages of my life. Not only that, I have come across the same thing in years of discussions with men, as well as during my research for this book. It is a general consensus among men that women will profess one thing, fail to totally meet the promise, then blame the man for them falling short.

Consider my close friend Jenny. She's a very active professional. Jenny works out five days a week, cycles and runs. She's also a very successful corporate executive. During virtually every conversation that we have, I can count on her talking about her need to find a "good man." A man that will treat her well and attend to her every need, a man that she can treat as her very own "king."

Well, as fate would have it, Jenny met Lawrence, a legal professional with a lifestyle similar to her own. With so much in common, they had a chemistry that was off the charts. They liked a lot of the same things and had many mutual interests that kept them engaged. Lawrence, so into

Jenny, started adjusting his busy schedule to make more time for them to share. Well, time moved on, as it does, and their relationship continued to grow. And while Jenny loved the idea of being in a relationship and having a man that loved her, Lawrence frequently expressed concerns about the balance in their relationship.

The problem was that Jenny had time to do everything that she wanted to do, but rarely enough time to do any of the things that she always claimed that she would do when she found that man that she could treat like her very own "king." In quite a few of their initial conversations they discussed the things that each person needed in a relationship. And while Lawrence worked tirelessly to do more, and give more than Jenny ever asked for, he often found himself at an emotional deficit. Jenny constantly told him how much she loved and appreciated him, yet there was always something that prevented her from fulfilling the most basic of relationship responsibilities.

During a recent conversation, Lawrence expressed dissatisfaction in the level of attention that Jenny had placed on the relationship. In an irritated rant he said, "Jenny, anything inside or outside of this house that needs to be done, I find a way to get done. Whenever you ask me to do something, not only do I do it, but I do it with a sense of urgency. We both have busy schedules, but why is it that I have time to invest in this relationship and you don't?"

Shocked and surprised, Jenny replied aggressively, "How can you say that? I love you so much and I do my best to tell you that often."

Expecting that response or something similar, Lawrence quickly retorted, "I don't deny that you love me in your own way, perhaps just not the way that I need to be loved. It seems that you have time to do everything but provide the intimacy that is a fundamental need and requirement for me. Why is that?"

Upset and on the defense, Jenny blurted out, "Well, if you were all the man that you think you are, just maybe we wouldn't be having these issues. Maybe I would be doing more, and feel compelled to do all of these things that you say I'm not doing."

Stop right there!

Let me get this right ...

- She said she wanted a "good man," a man that would treat her well and attend to her needs, a man that she could treat as her very own "king."

- She then meets a man that does all she asked for, and more, but she still fails to treat him the way she claimed she would.

- This man, who has exceeded her expectations, raises concerns about her failure to keep up her end of the bargain.

- She then rebukes him and blames him for her shortcomings in the relationship.

As bizarre as that sounds, that's pretty much the standard operating procedure for many women today. So, understanding this, it is incumbent upon men to manage our expectations of the women that we're in relationships with. Now, please know that I'm not saying that all women are defective in this regard, I am simply saying that there is a level of gamesmanship that women demonstrate in their attempts to secure male companionship. Considering this, men should enter into relationships taking a considerable amount of the pre-commitment pledges as empty promotional rhetoric, window dressing at best.

RULE 4.19: They Will Believe What You Tell Them

Have you ever been in a situation where you heard something that you knew was not true? I mean you were absolutely positive that what you were hearing was a lie. But you heard it over, and over, and over again. So much so that you found yourself debating whether you were wrong for your disbelief. But the lie, which was proven to be a lie, kept being repeated to you. Frustrated, you found yourself in a personal negotiation. You're not negotiating whether the lie is in fact a lie, but what parts of the lie might be true.

In time your mind moves from totally rejecting the lie, to searching for some part of the lie to believe in, to blindly accepting the lie as truth. So, what happens when you accept a lie as truth? Well, it's simple. You tend to adjust your behaviors to accommodate the lie. The problem is you can never arrive at a truthful or rewarding end because everything that you're doing is in an attempt to address, or acquiesce to, something that does not exist.

In or about 1977, psychologists introduced a term that they called the "Illusory Truth Effect." This term basically says that people have the tendency to believe false information to be correct after repeated exposure.

As men, we really need to be aware of this in our communications with our women. More specifically what we tell them, and what we attempt to convince them to believe. You see, we can constantly tell them lies, half-truths, or even paint a picture that may not be totally what we are making it out to be. And though their intuition may tell them otherwise, in time they'll most likely accept what we repeatedly tell them as truth.

But herein lies the challenge. What happens when the lie, the half-truth, or the partial picture is not what you need her to believe anymore? What happens when you actually need her to believe the truth? You can't have it both ways. So, it's important that you determine whether you want her to believe the truth, or the lies, because you can't sell her on both.

RULE 4.20: Create a Natural Option for Her

In the midst of a barbershop talk, one of the regulars, Fred, expressed a level of frustration with the relationship dynamics in his household. He said that every decision that he makes is met with opposition from his spouse. If he says "Up," she questions it. If he says call Terminix for the spiders, she'd call Acme Pest Control for the roaches. The conflict has him at an emotional tipping point – all he wants her to do is let him be the man. (Let him be the man?! RULE 3.13.)

Well, it would appear that Fred has multiple issues in his household. You see, the conflict and opposition that he faces is symptomatic of how his spouse views his leadership, or the lack thereof, in the household. I've said many times before that in the absence of a man, a woman will seek to fulfill that role. So, in this friend's case, the first question he needs to ask is not why there is conflict, but what is his role in the relationship, his role in the household? From the outside looking in, it is all too clear that the dysfunction is based on the lack of his definitive leadership role in the household. If he had such a role in place, she would not be so hesitant to follow his offerings and suggestions.

This is just one of countless examples of how conflict and resistance arises in relationships because what is offered up by the man doesn't seem reasonable, rational or safe for the household. To reduce issues like this, you must be able to create natural options for her. Or better said, making it easy to follow you.

Now, how is this done? Well, such a thing is accomplished by first establishing a solid leadership role in the household. Your leadership is demonstrated by what you do, as well as what you don't do – your ability to proactively solve emerging issues, as well as serving as the failsafe when things unexpectedly hit the wall. Once you earn the trust and confidence of that woman, she will naturally want to fall in line with your recommendations, not from a submissive standpoint, but from the view that she knows that you are making decisions that are in her best interest. Now this is not to say that she won't have questions or alternate options, but she will demonstrate a high level of confidence in your decisions.

Make it easy for her to follow you by creating natural options for her to choose.

RULE 4.21: Own Her Answer

I spoke earlier about being comfortable making tough decisions (RULE 2.5). This rule is related to that *Mannishlaw*. It has to do with making a decision that may not be your idea. Yes, there will be times when you will have to make decisions that you may not be prepared to make. And, in some cases, others will offer more sensible, more logical answers to address the challenges that you face. But it's your responsibility to determine the course of action.

This takes me to one of my earlier relationships, a time when I really didn't know what it meant to be a man. It was also a time before GPS and Google Maps. I was on a road trip with a young lady, coming up on an interstate interchange, and I was not sure about the direction. My memory told me to go to the right, but there was a lot of construction in the area, and I became indecisive.

The young lady told me to go to the left. She said that she had driven through there many times – it was definitely to the left. So I hesitantly followed her direction. To make a long story short, I should have gone right. Now we were lost and trying to find our way back to our original path. Frustration set in, and in a snappy exchange of words she told me, "Oh, you are the one driving, you're the man in charge, you should have gone the way your mind told you."

I have not forgotten this conversation to this very day. Now, if going left had been the right decision, we would have heard something along the lines of, "See, I told you we were supposed to go this way."

Here's the fact: It doesn't matter whether we went left or right. It matters that I failed to own the decision. See, when you own a decision, it's regardless of who offers the facts or the support. When you decide that the decision is to do something based on what somebody else says, you still own the decision. So, if things go well, you own it. But, if things turn out poorly, you still own that as well, because ultimately it was your decision.

RULE 4.22: Constantly Question your Optics

Here not too long ago I was having a conversation with a friend about how his poor choices were reflected in the eyes of those all around him. And as that conversation grew more intense I asked him, "Dude, you know what that looks like?" He replied, "I don't give a damn what it looks like, I'm going to do what I'm going to do. I'm right, and it has to be done."

The issue here is that of optics. The term "optics" applies to the importance of how things look, and how that may affect your mindset. It's important to constantly question your optics; that is, questioning the appearance of what you're doing or what you are engaged in. Whether it's your appearance when you walk out of the house, or how a clandestine meeting with someone could appear if it were not on the up-and-up. (Fact is, there are more issues arising out of homes because of misinterpretations and false assumptions based on nothing other than optics.)

Here are a couple examples of people making decisions based on how things appear, not necessarily how factual their thinking is, but essentially based on what they see.

- "I'm not eating that." "Why?" "It looks nasty." "Have you tasted it?" "No I haven't, but it looks nasty."

- "I'm not going there because it's in a bad area; I don't like the way the building looks." "Have you been inside?" "No, but I'm not going to an area that looks like that."

You should always consider your activities from the optical perspective of others. Ask yourself: If I were someone else looking at me right now, what would I possibly think?

Now consider optics in terms of relationships. How easy is it for you to be doing something that's perfectly innocent, but looks rather furtive? You know, for instance things like:

- Meeting up for happy hour cocktails with your spouse's best friend without telling her.

- Having a second cell phone ... for work, that your significant other neither knows about or has the number to.

- Taking trips or vacations with friends without your significant other's knowledge.

Now, while each of these examples can be very innocent, and have reasonable explanations, the optics don't look favorable. So, when making decisions, consider not only if it's right or wrong, but ask yourself, "What are the optics?"

RULE 4.23: Intimacy Impacts Expectations

Where exactly is the line that separates friends from being something slightly more than friends? Though I'm not exactly sure, I am positive that a line does exist, and it's often crossed without intent.

This subject came up doing a young men's mentoring group that I'm involved with. During a discussion, one of the members asked me why it is so hard to just be friends with women. He went on to say that he had a friend that he enjoyed spending time with, but she always behaved like they were more than friends. He intimated that this made him feel uncomfortable at times. Not in the sense of feeling physical or emotional distress, but uncomfortable in the sense that he wanted to be friends but have the flexibility to go out with other women.

Doing everything that I could to measure my response, and answer appropriately, I asked if they were in a dating relationship?

He quickly responded, "No, we're just friends, we just hang out." I then asked if she ever heard him refer to her as "just a friend." Again, he replied no, but not because they are more than friends; the situation had just never presented itself for him to answer that question in her presence. So finally I asked, "Have you done anything on a level of intimacy that is beyond what you do with any of your other platonic friends?" At this point he lowered his head slightly and said, "Yeah, actually we have."

Okay look, in relationships, there are some areas that tend to be more sensitive than others. You have friendships where you go out, do things, and have a good time on a purely platonic level. And those friendships are great. But what happens when intimacy finds its way into the friendship? Well, the expectations of the woman will often change. And honestly, they probably should.

Once your friendship graduates to a level of intimacy, you have officially left the realm of "just friends." Intimacy impacts expectations.

RULE 4.24: A Big Tool is Just a Big Tool

As crude as it may sound, this next Mannishlaw is a real thing that we must speak on. Too many guys are so easily puffed up and manipulated by our egos. And as a result, all too often, we find ourselves making bad decisions driven by our need to continuously feed our ego.

No one understands this better than women. And when you think about it, what can puff up guys more than anything else? Well, it's not his car, it's not his money, it's not the things that he's accomplished. The thing that can inflate a man's ego to infinity, and beyond, is for someone to say, "Wow you are huge! You really rocked my world." For a man to be told that he is well-endowed, or exceptional at satisfying a woman in bed, it's ... well ... a badge of honor on a level that very few things can touch.

There are men that will be okay being broke, generally recognized as being ugly, and having no discernible life accomplishments just as long as they can be recognized for having a "big tool." However false, it creates a pecking order of importance in the minds of some men. It impacts how they carry themselves, how they feel about themselves, and everybody else. The problem with this is, they tend to allow this feeling to have application outside of the bedroom or the bathroom.

What I mean to say is, it creates a mindset that, all too many times, make guys think that their gift of endowment, or ability to please a woman in the bedroom, is a remedy for all things wrong in their life or relationships.

I've heard men say things like:

- "I'm not worried about her. She knows how I rock her world."

- "I am about to go and break her back, and she'll shut up."

And to some extent, that may be true. She may never find another guy as "good" as you in the bedroom, or that makes her feel exactly the way you do. But one thing is for certain, she'll find many other guys willing to audition for the role, because there is no shortage of men willing to demonstrate how good they think they are in bed.

Here's the point: The size of your "tool" or your ability to please a woman in bed has very little value outside of the bedroom, and will rarely have any relatable impact on normal life issues. Simply put, a "big tool" is just a "big tool."

RULE 4.25: Know Your Net Worth

I was having a conversation recently with a group of middle-school boys. We were talking about financial responsibility. How to make money, save money, and grow money. We then started talking about the term "net worth." One of the boys Googled the term and came across a few celebrities. The conversation then turned towards who had more net worth than the next person. It was amazing to me how involved these boys were with knowing about the wealth of these celebrities. They even got into low-level disagreements about who they thought had more net worth.

After observing the conversations for a few minutes, I posed a question to them: "Which one of the celebrities is worth more to you, and why?" Note, I didn't ask what any one of these people had done to positively impact the lives of anyone in the room. All the boys stared at me with a blank look, then one held his hand up and said, "Well, outside of entertaining, nothing."

I then responded, "Then the answer is nothing, because entertaining is how they make their money." So I challenged them to re-frame their thoughts on net worth, splitting net worth away from wealth. We then defined net worth as your ability to positively impact the lives of the people around you. And what we soon discovered was interesting. The boys concluded that people can have substantial wealth, yet very little net worth. Conversely, people can have substantial net worth, but very little money.

I use this example to say that you need to know your personal net worth in terms of how you impact the lives of people around you. Are you contributing things that allow them to grow and prosper?

Go a step further – consider your net worth as value for the space that you occupy in the world. If you think in those terms, you will quickly recognize that there are some people who, if they were to disappear, no one would miss them, think about them, or even pick up a finger to report them missing (regardless of their wealth). Then, on the flip side, there are other people whose short absence can adversely impact the lives of many. Some of the people I've seen who have the greatest impact are those who have the least amount of wealth.

As a man, you must always seek to know, and to grow your net worth.

RULE 4.26: Get Yours, Don't Covet Hers

If you ever have the opportunity to query anyone that I've been in a relationship with, on any level, they'll probably tell you that I always tried to be their number-one fan and supporter. I genuinely enjoy watching people grow, achieve, and become successful. So much so, that I do my best to constantly encourage them to grow and prosper beyond their own vision. I celebrate their wins, but marginalize their failures.

That being said, I don't spend all of my time praising the accomplishments of others while doing nothing for myself. But there seems to be an emerging movement afoot. More and more I'm observing a growing subset of guys that are spending way too much time bragging on the women in their lives – their success, wealth and accomplishments – while doing absolutely nothing for themselves.

Case in point: I'm walking out of one of the city's most exclusive restaurants. On the way to my car, I pass a patio. There's a couple having afternoon cocktails, and the lady in the couple complimented my car.

She said, "I really love that car, I'd love to drive it."

I proudly responded, "Sure, you can drive it, but I'm going to need you to take the note as well." I said this with a light-hearted chuckle.

She responded with a laugh but saying, "I just want to drive, and I don't want the bill."

Oddly enough, at this point her companion felt the need to correct me, or enlighten me on her financial health. He proudly said, "Hey, don't think she can't afford to take the note. She makes a lot of money – you see what she's driving over there."

Both she and I looked puzzled for a few seconds, before I responded by saying, "Sir, I have zero interest in her ability to pay for anything, let alone your meal. I'm simply having a little humor about her complimenting my car. Have a nice day." This is just one example of what I'm talking about. This guy felt the need to brag on what she has. Not what he has. But there are plenty of other examples just like this.

I often find myself disappointed when I see things like men who feel really good about driving their ladies' car around town while she's hard at work. Or, you have those that absolutely love hosting events or inviting friends over to their ladies' homes, so they can show it off.

Again, please don't think I am being critical of one's right to be proud of the accomplishments of their companion. I'm just saying that it's not healthy for your relationship if you're constantly harping on what she is doing. At some point she is going to question why you are so concerned about her accomplishments, yet have little to show for yourself.

RULE 4.27: Don't Insult the Intelligence of a Scorned Woman

Relationships are complicated, and sometimes despite our best efforts, they don't end up the way we plan. So yes, you can be angry. You can be disappointed, disillusioned, devastated. You can be all those things when your relationship comes to an end. You've got a right to be; relationships are tough. But what you can't be, is on a vendetta against everybody that's in your future because your past relationship left you feeling destroyed.

Case in point: My buddy Romey and I don't agree a lot, but he's one of my closest friends. Some years ago, Romey went through a terrible breakup. Sonya, his then girlfriend, left him one step shy of being totally destroyed, decimated even. Some people get over things in time, and others just move on. But not Romey. He was a man scorned; he was destroyed. After he recovered from his breakup, Romey had one cause going forward, and that was to wreak havoc on anybody that wanted the "happily ever after" relationship. We started calling him the "Love Nazi." For example, Romey goes out of his way to date women, get in close, meet the kids, do things with the family, take trips and excursions. Then, as soon as he has enough indications that the woman is "all in," he goes cold turkey. And that's not just with one woman. He'll string four or five along simultaneously, just so he can go cold turkey on them. (He calls this catch and release.) He does this so they can feel the pain that he felt when his ex destroyed him.

Fast forward, and you have a destructive behavior going on. Behavior that yields nothing but broken hearts.

One day he and I were at our favorite spot throwing a few back like we always do. I happened to see one of the women of his past and asked him about her.

"Oh yeah," Romey said, "that's number 355. I caught and released her" on such and such a date.

Time goes by, and we're laughing, having a good time, and then I noticed that woman 355 was with about four other women that look eerily familiar. I leaned over to Romey and motioned to them. He said it must have been a reunion, that he had caught and released all of the women at the table. At that point I thought our situation could not have been good. What kind of coincidence is it that the last five women he'd dated knew each other. A while back I had told him that he needed to stop bringing different women to the same place he hung out, because if things went sour he'd set himself up for some sort of confrontation.

His response, "Look, I'm not worried. I want women to see me and then realize what they almost had, but won't have any chance of getting."

Now, this is where the craziness begins. Just as he was finishing his comment, all of the women got up and started heading in our direction. I knew it was absolutely time for me to exit. So I got up, left my money on the counter and migrated towards the door. One of the women called out, "Jerome!" Romey didn't react, he acted as if he didn't know her. Again she said, "Jerome! I know you hear me." At this point, with five women standing over you at the bar, with fire and hatred in their eyes, there are two things you can do. First, you could pleasantly greet them and say, "Ladies, good to see you. Let me buy you a pitcher, and we can sit down and have a conversation." Or, you can run. In this case, either of these things would have been appropriate. But neither happened.

Instead, Romey looks at the women and said, "I'm sorry. I am here on holiday. I'm not from this country and I'm having a hard time understanding you because I don't speak English." Well, because of the ensuing ruckus, the place is now under renovation, so we can't meet at that spot for a while. Plus, he's now staying with his mom, because somebody torched his house. More than that, he can't even drive, because his hands and legs are both in casts.

So, long story short ... there's a lot you can do in the wake of a breakup, but what you can't do is insult the intelligence of a woman scorned.

RULE 4.28: Don't Minimize Her Purpose

I think it goes without saying that people like to feel valuable, important even. When it comes to relationships, this point cannot be overstated. Now that being said, it's important to understand that we must get in the habit of treating people the way they want to be treated, not the way we'd like to be treated. This is a hard lesson that I learned not too long ago.

Take my girlfriend Denise, for example. It seems like we've been together for a lifetime. First kiss, 5th grade. And it's been a rollercoaster ride of sorts ever since, but you simply do what you have to do, to make the relationship work.

Well, a few weeks ago Denise walked in the room and told me she was concerned about her spiritual relationship with God, and she really wanted to work on her salvation. I told her I could support that, I understood. Everybody deserves a comfortable afterlife. But when she began to escalate the intensity of the conversation, I grew extremely concerned. She went on to tell me that we couldn't have sex anymore, unless I married her.

My response: "What? We've been together all these years, have all these kids running around here, and you didn't have a problem then. Now, all of a sudden, I've got to marry you? Well, I can't do that.

"Number one, because you're twisting my arm.

"And Number two, my wife would kill me if I came home and told her I married you – so that's not going to work!"

She walks off, pauses, then turns and says, "Look, it's all about sex with you. You're just using me for sex."

I just looked at her and replied, "No, it's not all about sex. I'm not just using you just for sex ... just mostly."

The isolated moral of this rule is that you can't make a woman feel pegged to serve a particular purpose. When you do, they begin to feel as though they are good for some things, but not others. They begin to feel minimized. And, it's when they feel minimized that they feel the need to demonstrate their value to you, in ways that you'd prefer they didn't.

RULE 4.29: Relationship Congruency

I'm probably one of the least critical people you will ever meet. People would say I'm a thoughtful person. In fact, in the course of the day I spend anywhere from eight to ten hours just empathizing with the plight of others. Of course, every now and then I come across some foolishness, which jeopardizes the sanctity of manhood, and at that point I have to call it out. This leads us to this rule on "relationship congruency."

The term relationship congruency seeks to satisfy an observance that I've experienced in the last few months. It deals with guys dating above their heads, or getting in relationships that are outside their capacity to manage. Relationship congruency can be defined as: When what you have to offer is in line with what somebody else's expectations are. We talk about this concept briefly in RULEs 4.2 and 4.3. Here we'll continue to discuss three vital areas that must be satisfied: financial, physical and intellectual.

The financial piece is something that lags and lingers. If you are not able to meet a woman's expectations financially, there's a lagging, lingering effect that causes you to revisit the same money-based issues on a regular basis.

Here's a key example: You're already working two-and-a-half jobs just trying to get your license back, because you're nine months behind on child support. *Anthony Hamilton*'s coming to town, and your girl wants VIP tickets to the concert. You want to take her, but it's $150 for tickets, plus you have to eat – by the end of the night you'd likely spend upwards of $500. You tell her you'd really like to take her to the concert, but you just can't swing it, you just don't have the funds. She may tell you with a smile that it's okay. But she's not going to do that for every concert that comes to town. So that's the financial piece of relationship congruency.

Now about the intellectual aspect. There's a lot that transpires outside the bedroom. We all know that sex is typically a vital part of a healthy relationship, but when you're not doing that you've got to do something called communicating. You've got to talk about things, you've got to be able to effectively communicate, whether it be about dinner, the current political climate, or the traffic commute situation. If your mate wants to have any kind of in-depth conversation – but all you can comprehensively discuss is *Call of Duty* or *NFL 2K19*, you're going to have a rift, you're going to have a lot of lost interest because you don't have the intellectual capacity to satisfy her needs. Intellectual capacity is something that's built over the years. If there's an intellectual gap, that's going to be a relatively substantial problem that I really don't know how you can overcome.

Lastly there's the physical component. Some people say that physical intimacy, sex, and physical attraction is not a huge thing for a good, lasting relationship. Sure, it's not a huge thing until it is the thing. If you're in a position where what you have to offer is lukewarm attraction, with okay satisfaction, she'll probably still be okay. Right up until Sir Lancelot, from the Kingdom of Three-Legged Men, walks up and offers her what she's looking for.

When you wrap all three of these components together, you have relationship congruency, or lack thereof.

All too often guys find themselves doing everything they can, just to hang onto a woman that clearly outclasses them (see RULEs 4.2, 4.3 and 5.9). These guys are clearly above their head.

In these cases, what can you expect? Well often women will just go along with the situation until it reaches a tipping point, or the relationship stalls. Eventually, whether actively, or passively, they'll start looking in other places to find the things that are missing in you. Then you're left with a relationship that ends badly, or, even worse, a bad relationship that simply won't end.

Guys, make sure you have relationship congruency. If you don't, your entire relationship will be a perpetual struggle. When dealing with women you don't have the capacity to sustain, you get to the point where you have to cut bait. You can't keep the relationship healthy, or whole, because you're doing your absolute best just to be in the relationship. And, I think most would agree that just being in a relationship is not the brass ring that most pursue.

Don't be a placeholder that keeps another, better qualified man from making a better life with that woman.

RULE 4.30: Relationships Can't be a Struggle

In a recent conversation, one of the deacons at my church told me he's crazy about a woman in the church's congregation. He said that they had been quietly dating for almost a year. And while there's so much about her that he absolutely adores, he feels that every passing day is becoming a greater, and greater struggle just being together. They're frequently arguing and fussing ... in and out of a cycle of fighting and making up. I listened, giving him ample opportunity to vent and share all of the relationship stressors that were hanging heavy on his head. When he was done, he asked, "What do you think I should do?" Now, anyone that knows me will tell you that I always resist giving people direction in making relationship decisions. I prefer asking questions and allowing them to come up with the answers themselves. And that's exactly what I did in this case. I asked, "If you don't have this relationship, what do you lose, and what do you gain?"

He stood in silent contemplation.

The point is this: A healthy relationship is about people getting together to create something more substantial than they could as individuals. If you're together and you're working on getting a house, or you're just dealing with the struggles of life, or perhaps working on creating a family – the good times are supposed to be even better because you are together. That's what happens when two people are in a healthy relationship. And even when the bad stuff comes, you've got someone to help you get through it, to take the edge off. They're going to ride or die with you.

Now here's the thing. If you're talking about being in a relationship, where the relationship itself is the struggle, well that's just problematic. You just can't do that. You can't be in a relationship and every day you're fighting and arguing. You're just surviving to be in that relationship.

Simply said, if you have to fight and struggle just to be in a relationship, then you have to seriously re-evaluate your position. You've got to ask yourself what it is about that person – and, what is it about you – that makes you want to be in such a relationship. You can't struggle just to be in a relationship.

RULE 4.31: No Domestic Abuse

How many of us haven't found ourselves in situations where firm opinions escalated into all-out arguments? In personal relationships these arguments can be especially sensitive, because subtle things can be said in the heat of disagreement that are extremely difficult to recover from.

Take my friend Jessie for example. He was upset, sick and tired of his bank account being overdrawn. He was tired of being broke every time he turned around, even while he worked three jobs. One day, in the heat of frustration, he told me that he was going to "go home and handle this situation."

Well, "going home and handling a situation" could mean a lot of things. But in this particular context I was a little concerned. So I asked him what he was about to do. He said, "I'm about to go home and tighten her (Keesha) up."

"Tighten her up?"

He said, "Hell yeah, I'm sick and tired of this."

Fast forward three days later. I see this guy in the grocery store. I was there getting things for my meal, when I saw him there walking around aimlessly, looking a mess. His eye socket was all black, stitched up, stitches all over – his nose, his lip, scratches all across his face, neck and arms. He was just looking a mess.

I said, "What the hell happened to you?"

"Man," he said, "you're not going to believe what happened the other day."

I said, "Looking at you, one of two things happened. Either you got mauled by a sleeping bear, or you went home and jumped on Keesha – which is pretty much the same thing as getting mauled by a bear."

This dude looked at me and said, "Man, I was going to go home and have a nice conversation with Keesha. I was hoping to bring her around to my position. But those damn kids left that skateboard in front of the steps. I slipped on the skateboard, fell up the steps, and as I was trying to get my balance, I fell on a rose bush ... that's how I got all these scratches. And then I hit my face on the steps going into the house."

"Wow man," I said, "I never knew a skateboard could be so hazardous to one's health ... if I believe that."

Look, it doesn't take a rocket scientist to figure out that this brother went home to jump on Keesha. And anybody who knows Keesha, knows that her nickname is "Big Grizzly" and she was not one to be jumped on. We all must understand that this sort of thing happens. Sometimes in the best or the worst of relationships we don't see eye to eye. That's just a property of relationships. Even still, we cannot allow our emotions to move us to a place where domestic abuse happens. It is never okay to adopt a mindset where you feel comfortable just going home to jump on someone. Likewise, it is never appropriate to live in a situation where you are frequently, or even infrequently, being abused.

There's no room in a relationship for domestic abuse or physical altercations of any sort.

RULE 4.32: No Male Friends

The barbershop is one of my favorite places to go for a few reasons. First, I can always count on my barber giving me a fresh cut that makes me feel super good about myself, and secondly, there's always a conversation going on that makes one think, "Wow, is this where we really are in the world?"

And on occasion, you can expect to get into a controversial conversation about something that somebody did, about what somebody else said, and why it isn't right. To this point, I recall a very involved conversation about opposite-sex friendships in a committed relationship.

Now the conversation started because my barber said that he had just finished arguing with his wife. He said that he had grown irritated with men calling the house asking for her, so he confronted her on it. Her position was that she's always had guy friends, and she did not see that changing just because she was married. She then accused him of being insecure. It's safe to say that he never anticipated her to respond that way.

Insecure?! As you can imagine, her response was enough to send the guys in the shop into an uproar. Some saying that it is totally unacceptable for their women to have guy friends, others raising conditions to male friendships.

As this discussion is unfolding, a woman in the barbershop could not understand what the big deal was. Yes, a woman felt the need to violate the sanctity of our domain, but that's a whole different conversation altogether (see RULE 5.10). Her cluelessness further exacerbated the climate of the room. The majority of men in the room wanted to shout down their point, but they decided that we'd all be better served if I explained their position in terms that she could understand. So I did just that.

I explained to her that, for a woman, the term "guy friend" is just that. A friend that happens to be a guy. That's just what it is, for the woman anyway. But for us guys, it's totally different. We have our male friends, but we don't do female friends. Females are the ones who put us in the "friend zone." And we just think it's okay to be their friend, but the whole time we're just patiently waiting for an opportunity to be more. So we play the friend. We can even know that she has a man, and we're okay with that too, because we'll have the best vantage point to watch and wait for him to mess up. And he is certain to mess up. That's when we will slide in the back door.

She sat there silently with a disagreeable glare on her face. So I went on to ask, "You are an attractive woman, how'd you meet your guy?"

Reluctantly she said, "Truthfully, we were just friends."

Case closed.

But just to be balanced, I also asked the men in the shop how they met their mates, and sure enough, every other man said they were after the booty. They didn't succeed, they got "friend zoned," but they were cool with it because in the back of their minds they believed a time would come that they could "hit it."

Now that was me expressing the overall sentiment of the men in the shop. My position is a little more cut and dry. If you're going to be in a relationship with me, you can't continue to accumulate any new male friends. In fact, I'm going to be skeptical of the male friends you already have. Knowing what I know, I can't allow you to parade around as an appetizing piece of meat for these guys you call friends to silently stalk.

No new male friends.

RULE 4.33: You Can't Avoid Difficult Conversations

The front-facing camera on today's smartphones has got to be one of the most ingenious inventions ever made. But still, you have people not properly utilizing them. You have women taking 15, 20 selfies a day, and still walking out of the house looking like crap. What's worse, men are not saying anything. Look, I get it – as men, we want to do whatever we can to avoid confrontation with our women. So we won't say anything, or we'll just agree to say, "You look fine," when they ask how they look.

We have to stop lying to these women. Sometimes we just have to have the difficult conversation for the health and benefit of our relationships. If you love your woman, you don't want her leaving the house looking any kind of way. Sometimes you just have to step up and say, "Babe, that dress is probably not the way you want to go. It's fitting a little snug. What size is that, a size 8? Maybe you want to step up to a size 14, it might look a whole lot better."

For the health of the relationship, you cannot allow your woman to go out with these false self-perceptions. Step up, have those difficult conversations. You can't be afraid of that.

RULE 4:34: No Time for Life

I can't overstate the importance of clearly defining the parameters of a relationship in the beginning. Once you get on that horse, it's pretty hard to change midstream. Likewise, when you set a range of expectations with a woman, they're pretty much set in stone. So those things you start off doing, you had better know going forward that you're going to have to keep those things up at a minimum. Women look for patterns. That's what they do. And the first opportunity they see you change in any way, they make a mental note, then the second opportunity, and the third brings concern in their world.

One of the biggest mistakes that you can make with a woman is demonstrating that you don't have time for anything but sex. You are perpetually busy with one thing and the next. Work, life, busy with everything except for her – right up until you have an opportunity for sex. Then somehow miraculously you have 30 minutes to an hour available.

It doesn't take a rocket scientist to see what's going on. And believe me, most women aren't rocket scientists. But they have enough sense to recognize when you only want them for sex, or whatever else it is that you want them for. Now, if that's what your relationship is based on, then it's okay. But just know, if she has greater expectations than just sex, problems are on the horizon.

RULE 4:35: Love by the Numbers

To this point, we've talked about a lot of different things. Personally I'm hoping I haven't said so much that I've left your mind foggy. But rules like RULE 4.1: Date for Substance, not Circumstance, RULE 4.2: Compatibility Breeds Longevity, and RULE 4.31: Relationships Can't be a Struggle are areas that are vital to recognize if you want any chance of building a healthy, enduring relationship. Now I bring up those points because I think this next observation, while tangential, will pull in aspects of those rules.

So, I'll ask you this question, "How numerically sound is your relationship?"

Look, I get it, this question seems rather bizarre. But just the other night, I was watching a documentary on space. And during the show, one of the astrophysicists made the statement that math, or numbers, serve as the keys to the universe. He went on to say that there's nothing in the realm of our existence that is not impacted by math.

The statement got me thinking, what would be the impact to our relationships if we simply applied the concept of basic math to them, in terms of compatibility?

Consider that, in a relationship, if I have pluses, and you have pluses, then together we have a lot of pluses. We can move forward at an accelerated pace. But on the other hand, if I have pluses, and you have minuses, then we can't go forward. Not at all, at least not together. Because in this case, one person will certainly benefit much more than the other. And the combination of what they have will be less than what the greater person possesses.

Now take, for example, that we both have negatives, and we put them together. Now, not only are we not progressing, we're actually moving backwards. So I ask, if you apply this mathematical thought process to your relationship, in terms of finances, in terms of life experiences, or in terms of material possessions, how numerically sound is your relationship?

RULE 4:36: Go Slow for What?

One of the things that I enjoy most is having an opportunity to talk with my sons about basic life issues. They're at a point now that they think they know everything, about everything, based off that one bad experience that they had last year, last month, or even yesterday. Oh, what I wouldn't give to be able to go back in life to be where they are today. That being said, I have to tell you about the conversation that I had just the other day. I had the opportunity to dispel the myth of "going slow."

Here's the backdrop: My son was in a relationship with a young lady that clearly wasn't compatible with him. And what I mean by this is, though they had lots in common, their core characteristics often placed them in conflict. I'll avoid any of the gory details, but what I will say is that the relationship ultimately ended.

So now, fast forward and my son has matured a little bit, has had a few more life experiences, and found a new friend. He tells me that he's not going to make any of the mistakes that he made in the previous relationship, he's going to avoid those problems. So I asked, "How are you going to do that?"

His response, "I'm going to go nice and slow."

"And that will do what exactly? Going slow, I mean."

"It will help me avoid the problems that I've had in the past."

I share this example because this is nothing new. How many times have we seen people come out of bad relationships, and their new thought process for future relationships, or just the next relationship, is to go slow. As if "going slow" is going to allow you to avoid any problems on the horizon. Let me ask you this, which would you prefer:

- To move through traffic quickly, or slowly?

- To get your job done at work fast, or slowly?

- To discover that you have cancer and need treatment quickly, or slowly?

- To find the person of your dreams, that potential soulmate, fast, or slowly?

I ask these questions because in our various life experiences, we generally want to get to the bottom line quickly, rather than slowly. And while this is not absolute, more times than not, there is a value, or a benefit, whether monetarily, physically or emotionally, to getting things going quickly.

If this is indeed the case, why on earth would we want to go into a relationship slowly? The truth is, adversity is unavoidable. You can't stop it. You can only deal with it to the best of your abilities. So if problems and challenges are going to come, do you want to recognize them and deal with them quickly, or slowly? Even to the degree of establishing or validating trust with a person. If you believe that "going slow" can allow you to uncover any issues or any gaps in one's character, then you must also believe that going slow can allow issues to metastasize, and character flaws to be better concealed. Consider this: The slower you go, the more time a person has to lie, cheat and deceive you, as well as cover their tracks.

So while there is something to be said for going slow in some areas, I'm not so sure that establishing a relationship is one of the areas that will be most beneficial in applying this thought process.

RULE 4.37: She's Not Your Everything

Love is a powerful, yet peculiar thing. It manifests itself in so many different ways, and affects people so differently, that I often wonder how so many different people can call love by the same name. I mean, how can one man take a life, and another man sacrifice a life, both in the name of love? Love is also tricky. I say this because it often gives us a glimpse or simply a taste of something that is so incredibly desirable, that it's hard for us to ever imagine life without that ongoing feeling or flavor. I guess you can liken it to an addictive high.

The tricky part of love's euphoria is that it often makes us see people in a way that is inaccurate and truly unfair to them, and to us.

"She's my everything."

That's how a heartbroken friend of mine described his ex-wife. He said it over, and over, and over again as he was weeping in my living room. They'd been together for years, and as much as he loved her, she found herself needing more. Something more than he was able to offer. And despite their best efforts at counseling and other activities intended to boost the health of the relationship, they reached a point where she needed to be free.

And still, all he could say was, "She's my everything."

I share this example because love often makes us feel like the other person is indeed our "everything." When the truth is, that mindset is improper, inaccurate and just plain unfair.

No one can be, or should be, responsible for meeting all of our needs. Think about it. That is a lofty expectation that is unfair to place on anybody. Yet many of us fall into that trap. Here's the problem: When we look at people and condition ourselves to feel as if this person is our world, whenever they cease to hit the benchmark, or meet our expectations in a particular area, the level of our disappointment can be tremendous. And sometimes the disappointment is more than the relationship can bare.

So consider this. When we think back to our discussions on compatibility, perhaps we need to stop looking for people that we consider our everything, and look for who can be our "important thing." Who can we expect to be in a position to meet those key needs that are most important in our life? When we have people in our lives who we can count on to be there, and who are able to supply our needs in the big, important ways, the trivial things become that much smaller in the overall scheme of the relationship.

PART FIVE

HOW YOU ALLOW HER TO TREAT YOU

One of the overarching goals of this book is to convey the message that men are known by manly behaviors. As previously stated, I believe that how a man treats himself typically has some correlation to how he treats others. But even still, there's another parameter that we need to consider – how a man allows others to treat him, women in particular.

We talked earlier about the rib complex (Part Four Introduction), how a man protects the rib, because the rib protects all that's important to the man. And while that's all good, we also emphasized how important compatibility is. But now, let's consider what would happen if the rib started to work outside of its purpose. What I mean is, instead of protecting the vital organs, the rib expressed a desire to think for the body, or see for the body, or any number of other functions that other organs are already designed and purposed for. Listen, I understand that this is an example that may be a reach for some to comprehend, but I use it to speak to behaviors that commonly transpire in relationships.

I like to call it, "role reassignment and conditioning." In RULE 1.1, I intimated that in the absence of a man, women will attempt to morph themselves into the vacant roles. Not only then, but in some instances women will either passively or actively attempt to change a man's role in the relationship, or displace him altogether. When it becomes necessary to fit their narrative, they'll attempt to condition men to adjust their relationship role, and even their all-around standards and expectations.

As men, it's our responsibility to set the workflow in the relationship. Without question, we must be the leadership voice and focal point. When we fail to do what is required to check these boxes, by default, we start forfeiting that leadership right and position. And with a woman, if you relinquish an inch, she'll seize a mile. Anything relinquished will almost certainly take an act of war to regain.

So with these thoughts in mind, I want to address just a few examples of rules that men need to understand. These rules will help us better determine how we allow women to treat us as men.

RULE 5.1: You Can't be an Option

I remember a time, way before now, when dating was so simple. Even enjoyable. I'd basically see a young lady that I was interested in, then wait for opportunity and courage to converge. I'd then approach her.

I'd say, "Well hello ma'am, I'm Solomon. I couldn't help but notice you from across the way. I didn't want this moment to get away from me without taking a second to speak."

Though my introductions were always basic and non-threatening, they usually led to small talk. The small talk always created an opportunity for me to make "the ask."

You know, "the ask" – I'd ask for her phone number, which would lead to more talking, which would most likely lead to the date. Keep in mind, this was a simpler time, so the date, or the first time we'd go out would most likely be something like Skate World, or the movies. I always preferred the cinema over on the corner of Dauphin and Sage Avenue. From that point, the relationship would run its course. Dating was so simple then. Almost as simple as connecting the dots.

But then came now, the present day. And oh, how things have changed. How can I best describe the whole dating scene now? Well, in a word, painful. I liken the dating scene to interviewing for a job that you absolutely don't want. You apply because you need a job. You get the interview and all during the process you smile, and you act as interested in the job as possible, all while the prospective employer grills you with all types of questions and "What if" scenarios that will never happen. In the back of your mind you're thinking, "F$%^, I hate this job already," but you must endure this process. You've got to listen to why this company is the best in the industry, why so many people are interviewing for this job, and so on.

And what happens? At the end of the interview, what do you do? You ask, "Do I have the job?" Now for you, emotionally, one answer is just as bad as the other. Because even if you get it, you'll leave the interview feeling like your new employer did you a favor by hiring you. You know, the whole "We could have hired anyone, but we chose you" thing.

If you're like me, then you've experienced a similar process. Perhaps you even felt or thought some of the same things. But the saddest part of the story isn't going through the interview. It's asking for and accepting a position that you know you don't want. What a flawed way of thinking.

Now I imagine by this time you're wondering what any of this has to do with dating? Well, I'll tell you. The current dating scene is almost a mirror image of the previous example. The modern dating process has basically evolved into a bunch of interviews, and, unfortunately, women, more times than not, are the prospective employers in the interview. They'll ask a bunch of questions, and as usual, we men, will be ill-prepared to answer them. So we'll sit in the interview, or on the date, looking for the most agreeable things to say.

She likes books, so we like books. She loves to travel, so we love to travel. This process will last over a period of phone calls, texts and face-to-face events, and with any luck you get chosen. And just like in the job interview, she'll probably do her part to let you know how lucky you are that she likes you.

Men! That's just not how it's supposed to be.

Case in point: Some time ago I'd grown extremely bored with single life. I did not want to be alone any longer, so I decided that I would try to meet a few people. I signed up on a few Internet dating sites and tried to make a few connections. First off, that's where the pain started. Just looking at all of the over-inflated profiles and wading through the BS requirements that everybody places on everybody else, was enough to make me want to slit my wrists. But I digress.

Finally, I connect with a young lady, we'll call her Geraldine. I sent a brief message over the app introducing myself, and she responded. By the third message she's asking for my phone number. Well, that's a little bit different for me. Usually I'm on the chase. I'm the one asking for phone numbers. But nevertheless, we exchange numbers. Well no, we didn't exchange numbers – I gave her mine. Now here's where the landslide starts to form. Geraldine calls me, but initially I had no clue that it was her, because my phone rang from a private number. Generally if I get a call from a private number, I suspect it's a robo call or something along those lines. So I sent it to voicemail. But on this occasion, I received about four call backs from this private number. So now I'm thinking that it's probably Geraldine calling. I finally answer the phone on the next call, and just as I had suspected, it was indeed her. We greet and talk for a while. Eventually she asked when we were going to meet. Again, this was a touch on the awkward side to me, because I prefer establishing the timing and progression for the meetings and dates. But again, I flexed, and we planned a date. We had originally agreed to meet at this quaint little restaurant that we both were familiar with. But, right as I was headed out the door, she called and asked if it would be too much for me to pick her up. Too much? Not at all. So, I headed in her direction. Now, picking her up changed the overall logistics of the evening. Because she lived across town, I had to drive past the restaurant, then double back in a hurry to get there for our scheduled reservation.

We walked in, and the hostess said, "You're more than 20 minutes late, so we gave your table away. But you are indeed welcome to dine at the bar." I looked at Geraldine and asked if she was okay with that. She was, so we ended up having dinner at the bar.

In the course of our conversation and banter, I found myself actually settling down and enjoying the evening. Right up until she flipped the "minimize switch" – the switch that women will flip, from time to time, when they want to make themselves feel important, by minimizing you.

She started by saying, "You're really lucky. I usually don't allow guys to come to my house or pick me up on the first few dates." I had to pause before responding because I wasn't sure if this was a joke or not. So I responded with, "Thanks, I appreciate the opportunity to drive across town to pick you up, and bring you back across town, to have dinner with you. I guess I am the lucky one." We talked a bit further and she said again, "Boy, you're really lucky. I would never have dinner sitting up to the bar. I only dine at tables or in booths. It's just more ladylike." Again I responded, "Well, I guess I am really lucky to even be having dinner at the bar, considering we were late because we were traversing the city to get here."

So we continue talking through the evening over dinner, discussing a range of things, when finally we got to the part about dating status. I mentioned that I was single because I had probably not appreciated some of the women in my past to the degree that I should have. She then indicated that she understood, as she was single because she had met too many unappreciative guys, like me. We both laughed a little bit then

she said, "The truth is, I'm single because it's a choice. I don't need a man, I'm just choosing to have a man to occupy a portion of my life. If it happens, okay, if it doesn't ... okay. I'm just not one of these thirsty women you're probably used to meeting."

At this point there were only two things that I could say: "Check please!" I gestured to the waitress for the check and offered her my black AMEX card for payment.

"Leaving so soon?" the waitress asked.

"Yeah, there are some things that require my attention."

Geraldine stopped in the middle of cutting her well-done filet mignon steak, which was drenched in A-1 steak sauce, and queried me. "What is going on? We're on a date. You didn't tell me that you had something else to do."

I said, "Yeah something just came up that I must do."

Geraldine further pressed me, with a concerned look on her face, "What do you have to do that's so urgent?"

"Anything besides this."

"Well I don't understand. I thought we were having such a great time."

"Please enjoy your steak ma'am. Can you even taste it under all of the steak sauce?"

So now the check had been paid, we exited the restaurant, and we made the drive back to her place. No radio, no conversation. The car was filled with the sound of the tires over the pavement, and the rattling of the loose items in the trunk as I hit the seams of the highway. Just as we were pulling up to her apartment complex, she looked at me, reached over and touched my hand and said, "Solomon. I don't know what happened, but I'm sorry. I apologize if I said something that offended you. I'd like to see you again, but I need to know what's wrong if we are to ever have that opportunity again."

Looking straight ahead, not even affording her the respect of turning and looking into her eyes, I said, "Geraldine, I'm nobody's option. Can't be. Won't be. This entire evening you've told me how lucky I was to be in your presence from one example to the next. Then you topped it off by saying you're not looking for a man because you need one, you're choosing to have one to fill your time. Well, I'm just not that guy. Nor should you want me to be."

I share this example because given the opportunity, certain women will make you an option. They will choose you, or give you the impression that you have been chosen, and make you feel like it's a privilege to be with them. It just can't be that way. Here's what you have to understand: An option is something that's extra, something that can be done without. It's generally added for some type of perceived pleasure or convenience. So, if you are a man, you can't be an option. You have to be a requirement.

RULE 5.2: Her Persuader is Best

So what makes women all the same? Well, I'll tell you.

First, all of them will tell you that they're not like other women. Next they will do their very best to show you why they are different. Third, women will do their best to give you what they want you to have, instead of simply giving you what you want. And lastly, they believe that their brand of persuasion is better than any other woman's that you've ever met.

Now, what exactly is persuasion? I'll let you think about that for a moment, but for the sake of this rule, we'll just sum it up as how they leverage their womanly ways and abilities. But generally speaking it involves them identifying what it is that you want, need and enjoy, and overloading you with more of it than you can handle. And they're generally okay with this because they don't intend on providing these treasures and treats for very long, just long enough to get you to do what they want. But it's not quite that simple, as that would be some type of quid pro quo. And they don't want it to look like manipulation. What they want is it to be your idea that you changed your mind.

So again, they make themselves available and flexible to do and provide virtually everything that you need and desire right up until they need you to come around to their thinking. And then the next thing happens.

Now at this point, it doesn't really matter whether you acquiesce to their thinking, or stay firm in your position; the next thing is the same thing. If you are persuaded to change your position and move in line with what they're requesting, they're going to slowly close the valve on all the things that they were doing. All of those things that you thought you had an endless supply of will slowly go away. But suppose you stay firm in your original position. The same things are going to happen. All of the things that you enjoyed her doing and providing will began to disappear, except for now they're probably going to disappear at an accelerated pace. Understand that by design they never had any intention of sustaining their behavior. It was simply a means to an end.

Take for example my cousin Tony's relationship with his girlfriend Shannon. Over the last few years, Tony has been experiencing cycles of escalating tension with Shannon. The conflict stems from the fact that Tony is not committed to marrying her. In fact, it's just the opposite – he's committed to not ever getting married again.

Now, the fact that he has this position about marriage should come as no surprise to Shannon, because he made her aware of this when they first started dating. Tony stressed that under no circumstances would he get married, or even consider it again, after the experience he had with his ex-wife. Now he was more than happy to travel, live together, and do virtually everything that couples, even married people, do, but he was not inclined to say the words "I do" ever again. So Shannon, super infatuated with Tony at that point, said she was okay with his position.

Now fast forward over some years, and her career has expanded, her body is slowly changing, and even her life expectations are adjusting. Shannon wants to get married. In the beginning, as with many relationships, she would drown him in affection, intimacy and just all-out sex. He never had to ask for his needs to be met, never had to question whether they would be met, and never found himself in a situation where he was in want for anything relating to her. And just like he offered in the beginning, they traveled a lot, lived together and did all the things that married couples do. But, they just weren't married.

Quite frankly, this was a point of confusion for Shannon. She asked one day in frustration, "Tony, we are doing everything that married people do, why won't you marry me?"

Tony responded with a sense of indignation, "Shannon I don't even know why we're having this conversation. If you think I'm about to get married to you, or anybody else, you must have bumped your head, or think I've bumped mine."

And though these conversations didn't happen very regularly, when they did they were more and more contentious. Their relationship was now in a state of constant erosion. It went from:

• We love each other so much, we can't keep our hands off of each other, to

• We really enjoy each other tremendously, and we may hold hands sometimes, to

• I sleep in this room, and she sleeps in that room, and hopefully we don't get in a situation where sex is expected. But we do love each other.

As men, we must expect that all women believe that their version of persuasion is better than anyone else's. So much so that they'll oftentimes accept your answer, even when it is in conflict with their goals. They do this because they have every confidence that over time they can bring you around to their position. The problem is, when their version of persuasion has little to no impact on changing your mind, what you once saw as a warm, considerate and loving partner, you now may see as a tense, treacherous and vindictive woman.

And while many things can be extracted from this example, I want to lean on this particular point. You can't allow women to believe that their version of persuasion is best. You must always emphasize to them that your positions are what they are. Where you are flexible, you will demonstrate flexibility. But where you are not, she shouldn't attempt to change your mind.

RULE 5.3: Don't be Led Around by the "Good-Good"

I'm not sure how my life would change if I hit the Powerball Lottery. I know it would, but I just don't know what degree of lunacy I'd reach. I imagine that I'd probably even have to hire someone to stay close to me to keep me from losing my mind, buying everything that I wanted, and traveling to exotic places. A lot comes with having more stuff. The more stuff you have, the more responsibility and discipline you have to demonstrate.

I mention this because I overheard a guy say that he had come across the "Powerball of women." It made me take pause, so much so that I had to dip into his conversation and ask what he meant. Turns out, this brother was getting an unlimited supply of the good-good. He said that his woman was pouring it on him 25, upwards of 30 times a week. Now I'm no mathematician, in fact math is one of my least favorite subjects, but I do know enough to understand that 25 times a week adds up to be about 100 times a month. Now, like most men, I understand the value of really good "good-good," so all I was thinking was, "Where can I get a ticket?"

Then he told me that everything wasn't as good as it seemed. But from my vantage point, 25-30 times a week, seemed pretty damn good. It turns out that the relationship had a manipulation component the he was not comfortable with. Anytime he wanted to do something that didn't involve her, have an opinion that she didn't necessarily agree with, or wanted to go somewhere where she didn't think he needed to go, she'd give him a code for "no more good-good," by crossing her legs and looking away.

I told him that he could not allow himself to be manipulated like that, no matter how much he was getting, or how good it was. But, just to be sure, I had to ask him one more time, "25-30 times a week?"

"Absolutely, and it's by far the best experience I've ever had," he said with a look of disgust on his face.

Okay, so here is the dilemma that this man is facing. First, he is addicted and doesn't even know it. He is with a woman that is giving him a feeling that he absolutely loves, right up until she gives him the feeling that he absolutely hates. The problem is, the feeling that he hates is the feeling of being minimized and manipulated. He feels less than a man. And though she also gives him a feeling that he loves, it is not substantial enough to mask the pain experienced from the feeling that he hates. The only thing worse than experiencing the repetitive feelings that he hates is knowing that he's going to go back to her to get more of the feeling that he loves. And with every cycle of this love-hate addiction to the "good-good," he grows more and more disgusted with himself.

Now look, you can be led around by a lot of things in life: in my experience, the best two things are character and ambition. "Good-good" cannot be one. You can't allow yourself to base life or less-than-life decisions solely on the "good-good." It just can't be that good!

RULE 5.4: Respect My Space

A friend asked me for my opinion about his issue. He was pretty upset. He said he'd had a pretty heated conversation with his old lady because she had been snooping through his cell phone. She found out that he had been studying abroad. Personally, I couldn't understand why there would be any conflict about learning he was doing that; that's commendable. I know a few people who have studied abroad and it's really helped in their lives and in their careers. But that's neither here nor there.

The point of this issue is that there's a phrase "What's yours is mine." Women really buy into this and believe it. Basically it's saying that what you have, I have a right to it, too. While I can understand why women would believe this for things such as homes and cars, the phrase does not extend to all properties and items. Personal property like cell phones, locked compartments, locked doors, glove compartments, safes, under my side of the mattress – those are personal spaces, and personal items. Personal items offer the owner what is called "the reasonable expectation to privacy." So, if it's my personal item, my personal space, stay the hell out of it. Leave it alone. For those things, what's mine is mine.

Back to this brother, I asked what specifically was so upsetting to her in learning you were studying overseas.

"Overseas?" he asked. "What are you talking about?"

"You said you were studying abroad."

"No, man, I was watching this chick on porn. I was studying 'a broad.'"

'Nuff said.

Look, every brother has a certain expectation to privacy. To the ladies: Leave our stuff alone.

RULE 5.5: They Are Who They Say They Are

I once went on a blind date – which, as we all know, blind dates are tricky, you never know what you're going to come across – and I met this lady, and I must say, this blind date was the most amazing experience I've had in a while. First of all, the lady was very attractive, very intelligent, and the chemistry we shared was out of this world. It was like one ongoing conversation that just morphed into something else, and then something else. We were laughing and smiling in this really nice restaurant. It all was going well. What else could you ask for on a blind date? Well, how about a first "real" date?

I called the lady up and told her how much I enjoyed our time, then asked her if she'd be interested in going out and catching a movie, maybe a nice dinner and cocktails. She said, "That would be really great. But how about you just give me that money, come over here and I'll cook you a nice dinner and we can watch a Redbox. I've got an excellent collection of wine." I thought that was a little different, a little weird, but sure, why not? So I went over to her place and we had a great evening. So then, what's next? Another date.

I got off work, and I heard on the radio that Mary J. Blige was making a special appearance in town. I love Mary J., so I called her up and asked if she'd like to go. She said, "I love Mary J. Blige! That'd be great ... but, you know, you could give me that money and come over here. I've got all her CDs and a couple of DVDs. We could just have some wine and have the coziness of my apartment and have our own private concert." So I thought okay, I would go over, kick it, have a good time.

About a week later my boss called and said I needed to go on a business trip to a conference in California. It was going to be four days, staying in the Ritz-Carlton, all expenses covered. So I thought about calling up this lady to see if she wanted to come out with me. I told her I was going to be out there for a week at this lavish resort, why not join me? I'd take care of her plane ticket. She said, "That'd be great! That would be wonderful. But hey, you can give me that money and I'll take the Megabus out there."

By that time, I was detecting a theme – it was always about the money. What was going on? Time goes by, and I was pretty much settled into her tendencies. Then I was having one of those days when all I could think about was getting some "good-good"; that's all I had on my mind. So I went by her house, and she was in there cooking. I threw $200 on the counter and I grabbed her.

She asked, "What's that for? What're you doing?"

"Hell, I just gave you the money," I said. "I'm trying to get me some."

"What the hell? You think I'm a whore or something? You treating me like a prostitute, just giving me money and trying to have sex?"

I said, "What?"

"What do you think I am? You throw money on the counter and then –"

Then I told her, "If, every time I turn around, you're asking me for money before you do something, you can't get mad because I give you money to do something."

Bottom line is this: They are who they show themselves to be, by word, deed or action.

RULE 5.6: 50/50 Ain't Good Enough

One day my woman suggested that our relationship was in trouble and she feared that we weren't going to make it. She felt that the relationship wasn't equitable and as a result she felt minimized. She said that she needed more give and take. It needed to be 50/50 if I wanted to keep her in my life.

At that point I told her that I was really disappointed that we were breaking up.

"Breaking up?" she said. "You've jumped all the way to breaking up without even given what I had to say the least bit of consideration. I need more give and take. It needs to be more 50/50, and I don't think you have that mindset."

I replied to her in the softest way that I knew how, saying, "If the burglar alarm goes off tonight, you're looking at me. If the roof starts leaking, you're looking at me. If the grass needs to be cut, you're looking at me. If you need a back rub, you're looking at me. I don't care how little or big – everything that needs done in and around this house – you are looking at me.

"So considering this, you're right we don't have a 50/50 relationship. The best that we, as a couple, could ever achieve would be 51/49. Why? Because I'll always hold the right to break the tie. That's just how it is."

RULE 5.7: No More "First Times"

Truth be told, as men, sometimes our level of naivete is beyond the pale. So much so, that we need to have people in our lives that are concerned for our best interest. Whether friends, or family, we need people that will tell us the truth and call us out on our stupidity.

If you live long enough, life will provide enough experience to help discern the likelihood of "what is" versus "what's probably not." Or simply put, life will make you intuitive enough to call BS on a situation with the highest level of confidence. This rule is called "No More First Times" for a specific reason. But before I highlight the reason, I want to give a little back story.

We've all experienced "first times" for a range of things. But in life, the window for "first times" is relatively narrow. In fact, most fall within generally accepted time frames. You have a time frame for your first steps, your first words, your first kiss, your first time at ... well ... you know, your first love, and your first break up. But all of these things follow a range in life. What I mean to say is that you rarely see someone taking their first step at age 14, or speak their first words at 9. When we do see things happen like this, they are deemed irregular, or abnormal, and we rarely accept them as being okay. Even a first kiss at the age of 44 would certainly raise questions in the mind of the person that is kissing you. Now I raise these points as a backdrop to the story of a guy named Ted, from the barbershop.

Ted is dating my cousin Marie, and because Marie and I are relatively close, I told Ted on several occasions that I am really not interested in hearing about any of his relationship idiosyncrasies as it relates to my cousin Marie. For me, it feels like it violates some level of privacy between cousins. That being said, every chance that Ted gets, he's telling me something about him and Marie. How good life is. What trip they're going on, so on, and so forth.

One day, Ted decides to violate all that is sacred between cousins by sharing his latest experience with Marie. He tells me these things at the barbershop, while we're waiting to get in our respective barber's chair. He said that they were out, things turned romantic, one thing led to another and they found themselves in the middle of something. Now while in the middle of doing that something, he asked her to do something else. That something else was something that she claimed that she had never done before, but because he requested it she was eager to do for him. The fact that she had never done that something that he had requested her to do, caught him off guard. He thought, "Wow, this is beautiful. We're sharing a very 'first time' at doing something together."

After revealing the details to this ultra-private experience with my cousin, Ted looks at me and says, "I feel super close to Marie now. Do you think I'm crazy for feeling this way because of this experience?"

As I said to him in the past, I had zero interest in talking to him about his relationship with my cousin. But since I felt like my arm was being twisted, I offered my opinion.

I said, "No, I don't think you are crazy for feeling close to Marie following this experience. I believe that you are crazy because you believed that you had the experience at all."

He sat silently next to me, looking puzzled.

I continued to take the opportunity to lay out the facts and paint a picture of what was most likely to be the case. I reminded him that Marie is 52, been married three times, and has six kids from five different men. So when he said that they were in the middle of doing something, and he asked her to do something else, and she responded by telling him that she'd never done that something else that he requested, but she'd do it because he asked, I'm thinking the odds are she'd probably done that something a few times before. Now, I could be wrong, but I'm probably not.

Here's the thing. Women love playing the role of the vestal virgin. They love putting on a front of innocence and ladylike-isms whenever possible. Now no one is saying that there's something wrong with common-life experiences. But in the mind of a woman, the fewer things that I am willing to admit to having experienced doing, the higher my stock will be.

The fact is, the longer you live, the more relationships you have, the more opportunities you will have to experience the various "somethings" that are involved with relationships.

Understand that I'd never castigate a woman for having limited life experience in the realm of relationships. But, I would say that it's absolutely absurd to pretend that you have not been privy to certain experiences, all to project a false sense of self value.

Men, please know that your window for first times is narrow. Anything inside or outside of the box, as it pertains to relationships, will probably be exposed before you're 30. So if you're dating a 50-year-old and she says that she has never done something before, odds are she's lying.

There are no more first times!

RULE 5.8: You Can't Accept Their Stress

Here recently, I found myself in a precarious situation, defending men in general. I was attending a Women's Empowerment Convention. I usually try to attend two to three of these a year, just so I can stay abreast of what's going on in the female mindset. As men, we need to have some indication of what's going on in the heads of our women on a mass level. So I go to these conferences to just take the pulse of the female gender at large. What are they talking about? What are they concerned about? What new and evolving plights are they going to try and hang around our necks? And what have I learned? Absolutely nothing. Nothing new that is. Everything that they're moaning and groaning about is the same stuff that my great-grandmother, and her mother before her, moaned and complained about. But that's neither here nor there, because I knew this would be the case when I register for the convention in the first place.

So, 10 a.m. came and I found myself sitting down on the second row waiting for a panel discussion to start on the subject of "Women committed to married, or otherwise committed men."

Yes, that's what I said. Re-read the previous sentence and think on it for just a minute. Now during this panel discussion, I noticed a few common themes.

Theme #1: I deserve whatever I want, because I am making myself available to him.

I must tell you that I was absolutely astonished at the sheer number of comments associated with this theme. The general consensus of these women in the room was: If a woman enters a relationship with a man that is committed to someone else, then he has a certain responsibility to meet her needs. He must take care of them, on some level, without end. They should have no struggles, no financial woes, no disappointment, at least nothing that is within his reach to positively affect.

I raised my hand with a question during the segment. The moderator recognized me, and allowed me to speak, and I made my best attempt to offer a little clarity and counterpoint to the discussion. I told the ladies in the room that they should consider one thing, the financial limitations of the man. If every time you want, or need, or require something, and this man is there to spend, what is going to be left in his bank for his primary household. And even if that's not your concern, how concerned will you be when he's broke and has nothing to offer you at all? I could hear the mumbles and murmurs in the background, so I felt that it was time for me to take a seat. They moved on to the next topic, without even considering my points.

Theme #2: Stop trying to hide me.

Are you serious? Yes ... based on the conversations on this topic it would appear that one of the worst things that a committed man can do to the woman that he's dating on the side, is to act as if he's not dating her on the side. For some reason, the women in this room loathed the thought of constantly meeting their guy at obscure restaurants, social venues, and other places out of sight of most people known by either of them. Even though they are the secret women, they are insulted at being kept secret, or denied. Once again I thought my experience as a man might allow me an opportunity to contribute some very valuable insight. So I raised my hand and stood up. I asked them, "How beneficial do you find the relationship that you're in? Now, whatever the benefit is in the current state of your relationship, ask yourself how much more beneficial would it be if you added a stab wound, a gunshot wound, a court case, or anything along that vein? Because that's what you're going to add to the relationship if your guy doesn't keep you a secret from the person he's committed to."

Gentlemen, again, I offer no support for, or judgment against, anyone that finds themselves in this sort of situation. But what I will say is, you cannot allow your co-committed relationship to put undue pressure or leverage on you. In fact, the purpose of the extra-relationship is to bring relief and pleasure, or happiness to your life when the trials and challenges of the primary relationship have you stressed beyond measure. Regardless of the nature of your side relationship, it cannot serve as an additional stressor in your life.

RULE 5.9: A Spoiled Woman

It's my hope that as you read this chapter you don't build an impression in your mind that is all about negativity against women. On the contrary, these aren't opinions for, or against women, they're simply observations that I am stressing so that men can be better prepared to deal with these circumstances when they arise, and arise they definitely will. Now in fairness, when relationships falter and fail, it's usually not the fault of the women. Most often, we are to fault because we are so blind and stupid that we will not see the evidence, or the patterns that sit right in front of us that let us know that this woman may not be the one that we need in our world. Or just maybe, we need to make some adjustments so that we can better mesh with this woman, if we are indeed committed to a relationship with her.

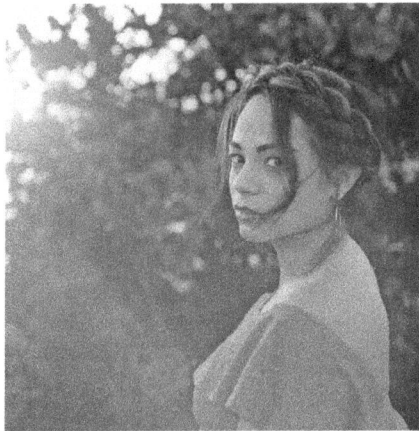

Now that being said, there is something called a spoiled woman. I'm not sure that all of you are familiar with the term, but spoiled is a description of the attitude. How best can I describe this to you? Well, let me put it to you this way: Typically a spoiled woman has an all-about-me narcissistic attitude that can cause her to demonstrate some sour, nasty and even disrespectful traits at times.

The problem with a spoiled woman is that the spoiled characteristic tends to land on a woman that is otherwise a great catch. She's probably relatively pretty or fairly intelligent. She may also have a few additional things going on, such as a strong career, or an entrepreneurial enterprise. But unfortunately, the spoiled part sours the whole package. A spoiled woman is like an opioid addiction. You know you don't need to be dealing with her, but you do because there's something about her that you enjoy being around. And you will be around her as often as you can, until the spoiled characteristic repels you. But, again you'll come back because you need to be around this woman. It is something about her that you enjoy so much. And she knows it. That's why she has no incentive to do or be any different.

Her all-about-me attitude will make you want to gouge your eyes and ears out at the same time. Her "I need this, I want that" disposition, with no regard to your financial or emotional state, will make you feel disgusted with yourself at your inability to pull away from her. The fact is, you'll never be able the satisfy her, and the things that you do for her will be treated as requirements. Little gratitude will be expressed, except for when it appears that you've reached your limit, and you're about to turn the faucet of giving off. But then, she figures out how to conjure up a few ounces of humility just to smooth over this rough patch in the relationship, only to quickly settle back into her normal role.

Men, a spoiled woman is by far the worst type of woman to deal with. She will fleece you both financially and emotionally. I don't care how attractive she is, or how good the "good-good" feels, as soon as you realize that you're dealing with a spoiled woman, you must break free. Don't walk, run! Don't try to understand her. Don't try and just be friends. Get away from her like you're getting away from Anthrax.

I can think back to my youth, when I was old enough to experience a woman, but young and dumb enough to think I actually understood her. I got entangled with a spoiled woman, and it was one of the greatest learning experiences that I've ever had, bar none. The needs that I had to satisfy for this woman were simply dangerous. I found myself doing, and being involved with, things that were reckless, disrespectful and just plain unsafe. And the thing is, she was okay with it. Because generally, I was only putting myself at risk. So if I had to put myself at risk to make her happy, she was okay with it. Thankfully I woke up when I saw the light. Now sadly, it wasn't the light of wisdom. Or even an epiphany that I had in meditation. It was the light that came from a muzzle flash after getting shot at. Now, I'm not going to go into the specifics of it, because we never know who reads these books, but what I will say is I found myself involved in something that I had no business being involved with, only because I had somehow become tied around the finger of a spoiled woman.

So if you find yourself with a woman of this type, how do you move on from them? Well, I'll tell you this – you can't wean yourself off of them. Like drugs, their grasp is too strong on you physically, and psychologically. You have to simply go cold turkey on them and get away from them. But even that's not enough, because there's virtually no one thing that you can do to overcome the gravitational pull of a spoiled woman. You literally have to have some type of combination therapy to overcome this problem. What I mean to say is, not only must you go cold turkey, but you must keep every waking hour of the day occupied with activity. Not empty activity like walking, or exercising, but activity that occupies your mind because what you can't do is get caught up in thoughts about her. You can't find yourself in that personal negotiation where you're wondering if you are really right to stand your position. You can't get caught looking at your phone every five minutes wondering if she's going to text you, and hoping that you don't get weak enough to text her. You can't find yourself going to hang out at the places that you know she typically goes, just for a glimpse. None of these things are acceptable, but they are likely if you don't have enough activity keeping you busy and engaged.

Even if you do, it's not a one-day thing. You literally have to have a wash-out period to get a spoiled woman out of your system. And when I say wash-out, I mean you have to go from:

- Craving her, to

- Needing her, to

- To occasionally thinking about her, to

- Being okay without her, to

- Being angry that you were ever involved with her, to finally

- Not thinking about her at all.

Now, let me warn you. You can be halfway through all of those phase progressions, and if you go back and deal with her on virtually any level, you're going to relapse, and have to start all over again. So, if you currently are with a spoiled woman, be ready; just know that life will not be good for you, it cannot be good for you. And if it is good for you now, you are just too stupid to realize how bad things are, or about to be.

RULE 5.10: Respect Our Place

Much like RULE 5.4 talking about respecting our space, we must also make it known to women how important it is to respect our place. For instance, recalling a time I was with my buddies at one of our favorite social spots, I told one woman, as a response to a comment from her, that just because you can go to a place, doesn't mean you should go to that place.

She had walked by, seeing our cluster of tables, and said, "Gentlemen, I happened to overhear your conversation, and I want you to know that I found it extremely offensive. In fact, just watching your behavior is disturbing – it's degrading to women as a whole."

My guys were blank, not knowing what to say. So I took the opportunity to speak on their behalf.

"Ma'am, why are you even here in the first place? The sign out front says 'Gentlemen's Club.' So why are you even here? In fact, with all the music and dancing going on all around us, how did you 'happen' to hear the details of our conversation?"

Here's the point: Whether it's a gentlemen's club, a straight-up strip club, a cigar bar, a poker or game parlor, a barber shop, a car or biker's club, these places are historically gatherings where guys get together and talk about what guys deal with or experience. These are places where men can talk without being on guard and making sure we deliver things in context in a way where it's tempered so no one's offended (the "no one" being women).

Now, I'm not so misogynistic to say that women should have a place – no, I won't say that. But what I will say is that guys should have a place. A place where we can congregate and be free to do guy stuff, to have guy talk, without women being involved with their opinions, their push back, and their positions toward how we should feel and how we should express ourselves.

Know your place, and make sure it isn't in somebody else's place.

CONCLUSION

The rules in *Mannishlaws* are not only the results of my personal observations, but also a compilation of generations of experiences shared by many men. Over the course of my life I have known people who have seen a lot, and I have seen people that knew a lot. And through the years, many discussions and personal life experiences have conditioned me to realize that these rules in *Mannishlaws*, while not absolute, are absolutely dead-on. They are real, and they are true.

Looking specifically at my life in totality up to this very moment, if I'm honest with you and myself, I'd have to share this testimony. The biggest disappointments that I have experienced were self-driven and self-inflicted – not wanting to listen to anything that was counter to what I wanted to do, or not wanting to do what was required when it conflicted with my personal program. These were the behaviors that led to my inability to hit the ball when I was up to bat.

Secondly, the biggest failures that I've experienced in life have been due to my inability to exercise good judgment with vision that extended beyond my fingertips. Living for "what feels good right now" created an environment that led me to exert enormous amounts of ambitious energy pursuing things that I did not need, only to end up with prizes and trophies that I did not want.

Then lastly, my greatest relationship failures and mishaps were because of my inability to walk within my role and responsibilities as a man in a non-deferring, non-fearing manner. Unable to be unwavering in a few instances when stability was required, has subsequently caused me to reap my just rewards in life.

Even when I consider my greatest successes in life, I've found that I struggled to enjoy or appreciate them for long because I have yet to free myself from the emotional shackles of my past failures and missteps. These emotional bookmarks constantly drive me to work harder, and harder for nonexistent recognition and validation. Always trying to convince myself that I am better than my mistakes.

If this book, with all that it shares and endeavors to impart, had been available to me 20 years ago, how much more would I have accomplished? How many fewer catastrophic mistakes would I have made? While that may be debatable, here is what's not – you don't have to experience everything firsthand to know whether it works. So take these rules for what they are, an opportunity for you to understand how to embrace manhood, live as a real man, and how to live a life at a higher level without regret.

STAY UPDATED!

There are constantly new and updated MANNISHLAWS rules online! We'd love to hear from you. Check out the MANNISHLAWS YouTube blog (just type in "MANNISHLAWS" in the YouTube search box).

Don't forget to like us on Facebook at **www.facebook.com/ mannishlaws2019/**

Order more copies of ***MANNISHLAWS: Manhood Defined*** directly at **www.mannishlaws.com/products**

www.ingramcontent.com/pod-product-compliance
Lightning Source LLC
Chambersburg PA
CBHW060847280326
41934CB00007B/957